The New Covenant
in the
Old Testament

Discovery Books

The New Covenant in the Old Testament

David H. Roper

Word Books, Publisher
Waco, Texas

Discovery Books are published by Word Books, Publisher
in cooperation with Discovery Foundation, Palo Alto, California.

ISBN # 0-87680-848-8
Library of Congress catalog card number: 76-5718
Printed in the United States of America.

With thankfulness
for the honey
that brightens my eyes.
1 Samuel 14:29, 30

Contents

111303

Preface

What is your understanding of the nature of the Old Testament? Is it a book of musty laws and mostly fulfilled prophecies? Is it a quaint historical account of a peculiar people, the Jews? (How odd of God to choose the Jews!) Is it a culture-bound volume of antiquities with a few useful poetic sections thrown in? Does it, in fact, have any major place in our lives today?

Christians have a special relationship to God the Father, and the basis of that relationship is God's own covenant, his promise, which he has sworn never to break. He will be our God, and we will be his people. He established that covenant with his ancient people, and as the Scriptures flow onward to the time of Jesus, the covenant which God initiated and sealed was expanded upon, repeated, and finally brought to ultimate fulfillment in Christ.

But from the beginning, the relationship man could have with God has always been the same: He has always extended forgiveness and the power to live free from sin, frustration, and defeat. His grace is eternal and has always been available to those who would entrust themselves to him. This relationship, which Christians call the New Covenant relationship, is spelled out, pictured, and sung about throughout the Old Testament.

I have written this book to try to convey something of the excitement and nourishing richness of the Old Testament as the Word of grace and truth. It has a different flavor and texture than the New Testament, of course; if the New Testament is bread and wine, the Old Testament might be considered meat and potatoes. Both are important for a balanced understanding of what God is trying to communicate to us.

I want to highlight the way in which the nation of Israel pictures the "New Covenant" in action. Fulfillment and victory for them are based wholly on dependence upon God as the only possible source for all that man seeks to do.

For me, the Old Testament has a very special appeal. The lives recorded there—the testimony of human weakness and of God's incredible patience and relentless love —speak eloquently, both of the character of God and of the inevitable perverseness of man seeking to live apart from him. I know my own perverse nature; I can identify with the failings of the Israelites. Seeing myself in them, I am struck even more powerfully with the parallel account of a God who continues to pursue his people.

This book is short; it could be much longer, but why spoil your fun? I hope you will be intrigued by what God is revealing in the Old Testament and be hungry for more. Once you catch just a glimpse of the personal and dramatic truth revealed in the Old Testament, you will be on your way to a deeper understanding of how to live out of the full provision God has made for us all in his eternal covenant.

—I—

Getting Our Bearings

Through an accident of history, the first thirty-nine books of our Bible are called the "Old Testament," and the last twenty-seven books are called the "New Testament." This division into two books, of course, is sound, based as it is on the radical division in man's history into the period before Christ's coming and the period after his coming. The dividing point, then, for history and the Bible is the incarnation. The Old Testament is the book of ancient Israel and looks forward to the promised seed of the woman who would crush the head of the serpent. The New Testament is the book of the New Israel—God's new community—and looks both backward to the Coming and forward to the Consummation of all things.

The two-fold division of the Bible is valid. However, the *terminology*, "Old Testament" and "New Testament," can be misleading! Certainly to think of the Bible *merely* in terms of an Old and New Testament may perpetuate what I believe is a widespread misunderstanding of the nature of the two Testaments. I am not advocating that we do away with this classic terminology. That would be both impractical and unnecessary. We are historically committed to it. However, we do need to understand that these are not biblical terms. The prophets or apostles never refer to either Testament as the New Testament or Old Testament (2 Cor. 3:14 is referring specifically to Mosaic Law). Their designation is normally "the Writings" or "the Scriptures." In other words, our terms Old Testament and New Testament are later titles that do not bear apostolic authority.

Now, let me explain my uneasiness about our use of these terms: Old Testament and New Testament. First, a point of clarification. The term "testament" actually means "covenant." The words are interchangeable. Our title for this book, therefore, is almost a contradiction in terms, since what we are actually saying is, "The New Covenant in the Old Covenant." The only difference between "covenant" and "testament" is one of derivation. Covenant is derived from the French *convenir*, while testament comes from the Latin word *testamentum*. Both words essentially mean an agreement or legal witness. The designation for our English Bible came by way of the Latin Vulgate and thus we got our titles, Old and New *Testament*, instead of Old and New Covenant, but the latter terminology would have served just as well since the terms are interchangeable. I don't know exactly *when* these terms, Old and New Testament, were first applied to the Bible, but I do know *why* the two divisions of the Bible were so designated. In the eyes of these early translators the first thirty-nine books dealt principally with the Old (Mosaic) Covenant and thus received the name Old Covenant (Testament). The last twenty-seven books were concerned with the "covenant in my [Christ's] blood"

(Matt. 20:28) and thus should be entitled the *New Testament* (Covenant).

It shouldn't disturb us greatly that the terms were applied and have continued in use. One can understand the thinking of these men, and their reasoning was valid. The Old Testament is an unfolding of the relationship of Israel under the Old Covenant. The New Testament does show how the New Covenant was mediated through Christ. The problem comes in thinking that the first thirty-nine books are *nothing more* (note the emphasis) than books of the Law, containing only introductory matters to the gospel. In other words, the terminology that we use to describe the two divisions of Scripture may reflect the erroneous notion that the New Testament is a book of grace and truth superseding the Old Testament—thus the Old Testament has no relevance for our life and experience as Christians. Because we equate the Old Covenant (Mosaic Law) and the Old Testament, we may see the Old Testament only in the sense that it is, as Paul said, a "tutor" (*paidagogos*) until the time of Christ (Gal. 3:24). In Paul's thought the Law restrained man until Christ came, and now that Christ has come and we are granted full sonship there is no longer any need for a "tutor." One cannot quarrel with his assigning to the Old Covenant a pedagogical function, for (or at least so I believe) it indeed had such a function. The rub comes in thinking of the Old Testament *exclusively* in this way.

The crux of this entire issue is a false equation of Old Testament and law. By making the Old Testament synonymous with law the two testaments stand in almost total discontinuity with each other. Law and grace are seen as antithetical, opposing principles. The Old Testament is law; the New Testament is grace. Thus the Old Testament has no practical function now that we live under grace apart from its antithetical portrayal of law. In other words the Old Testament is useful today only to the extent that it shows us how hard man had it under the law and thus we learn to appreciate grace. Thus, reading the Old Testament is like hitting oneself over the head with a hammer. It feels so good when you quit!

If the Old Testament is accorded only the pedagogical or antithetical function of preparing men's minds for the gospel or revealing by contrast the riches of God's grace, then the door is thrown open to an interesting question. Is the Old Testament really needed? Now that grace and truth have come through Christ, could the Old Testament not be dropped from our canon and something else substituted that would serve just as well? (I am told that the question has been asked and answered by certain churches in India where some have suggested that the ancient Hindu scriptures would provide a better introduction to the gospel for the people of that land than does the Old Testament.) The question, of course, is outrageous, but given an equation of the Old Testament and law, it is logical and sooner or later it is bound to be asked. In fact, it probably has on a practical level. Think for a moment: Of the fifty-two (give or take a few) messages you have heard in church this past year, how many were on the Old Testament? Can it be that our Old Testament–New Testament terminology reflects a deep-seated misunderstanding of the nature of the Old Testament which has in fact led us to a drastic devaluation of it? The question ought to be answered!

Now, will you join me in what may be for you a fresh look at the relationship between the two Testaments? First, we need to understand that the older books, although they certainly contain the law, are much more majestic in their scope and purpose. They transcend the law. The Bible is actually one book divided around the incarnation of Jesus Christ with a number of themes running throughout both divisions. Two of the major themes are law and grace; a fact that probably comes as no surprise to you. However, don't think of law and grace as opposing principles, with the Old Testament emphasizing law, and the New Testament emphasizing grace. Law and grace are not distinct periods running consecutively.

Rather, they exist as parallel themes running from Genesis all the way through Revelation.

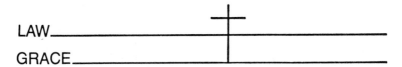

It's this premise that I hope to demonstrate in this book.

A Definition or Two

It is important to define the terms "law" and "grace" as I am using them. When I refer to the law, I am not thinking merely of Moses' Law, although it should be obvious to everyone that the Bible uses the term "Law" in that technical sense. But I am thinking of law in a more general way as the revelation of God's will and character which is expressed in a variety of ways in both the Old and New Testaments.

The initial expression of law in this sense was in the Garden of Eden where God revealed himself to Adam in the cool of the evening—a figure evoking the idea of a personal and intimate relationship. Adam knew God and God's mind. When Adam ate the fruit, he knew that the act was forbidden (Eve may have been deceived, but not Adam—he knew!) (1 Tim. 2:14). That communion between God and Adam affected the first revelation of the law.

After the Fall it appears that in general the line went dead. Few men experienced the personal communication with God enjoyed by Adam. They did, however, retain a racial memory of that relationship, a deeply ingrained universal memory of what used to be. (Rom. 2:15). Because of that memory, every man from the Fall to the present has a sense of what ought to be. Though it is less tangible than a written or codified law, it is nevertheless just as real and just as nagging to the conscience. The "law written on the heart" is a second way in which God's law is expressed to man. It is that law which makes people everywhere agree in general on what men and women ought to do. We do not agree in all the particulars, but in general we do know what constitutes true manhood and womanhood. For example, I know of no civilization that rewards and honors cowardice. Perhaps one exists, but if it does, I am sure most would agree that that fact in itself would suggest a declining society. Someone has commented that one would never clap an alligator on the back and say, "Be an alligator!" Not only would it be silly, it would be unnecessary. Alligators are almost always true to their nature. We do, however, at times admonish one another to "be a man," and we intuitively know what is meant by that statement. We know there is a standard of manhood that we have violated and need to be called back to. That standard, a vestigial memory from before the Fall, is the law written on the heart.

Years ago I recall seeing a segment of the TV series "This Was The Week That Was." David Frost was seated behind a card table interviewing the recently deceased. One after another they filed by, and having received a verdict on their destiny, each went through one of two doors—one marked "Heaven" and the other marked "Hell." One man seemed confused as he approached the table. "Which way do I go?" he asked the judge. "You know," David Frost replied. But the man seemed undecided, so he asked again. Once more David Frost replied, "You know." Then without hesitation the man walked through the door marked "Hell." That was a very trenchant moment in that program. It illustrated the profound truth that men instinctively know what they ought to be, and furthermore, that they have not lived up to that standard of excellence. That knowledge is law—the law of God written on the heart, and that expression of law is elucidated in both the Old and New Testaments.

When the law of God written in the inner man is projected outward on a larger scale, it becomes a third "law" —societal law—that governs communities and nations. And again, those laws are curiously similar wherever you go. They may differ in detail from place to place, but not in substance. Men in general agree that it is wrong to steal, murder, commit adultery, and covet one another's possessions, although they may differ in their understanding of the particular circumstances or times when those acts are illegal. Societal law is, likewise, an expression of the will and character of God. However, like the law written in the individual heart it is a distorted representation of God's character since it is always a mixture of truth and error.

The fourth expression of law is Moses' codification of the will and character of God in the Book of the Covenant. We do need to realize, however, that long before Moses wrote the Law on tablets men were aware of the truths contained in those laws. The Law at Sinai did not burst on the ancient world as an entirely new revelation. God had already written his law on their consciences. As early as 2000 B.C. (about 600 years before Sinai), the kingdom of Eshnunna (near modern Baghdad) published a set of laws very similar to the law revealed at Sinai.

> If a man gives money for another man's daughter but another man seizes her forcibly . . . and deprives her of her virginity, it is a capital offense, and he shall die.

In Eshnunna, the rape of an espoused woman was a capital offense (cp. Deut. 22: 23–27).

> If a man takes another man's daughter without asking permission of her father and mother and concludes no formal marriage contract with her father and mother, even though she may live in his house for a year, she is not his wife.

So in Eshnunna marriages were solemnized only by some form of legal contract. In other words, there were no common-law marriages. Further,

> If (a man) concludes a formal contract and cohabits with her, she is his wife; when she is caught with another man, she shall die.

Thus adultery was also a capital offense (cp. Deut. 22:22). In most respects the Laws of Eshnunna did not reach the high level of morality expressed in Moses' Law, and they were in general restricted in their application to the upper classes, but they do indicate the extent to which the Law of God had permeated society even before Moses' day.

It was Moses' task to transmit the codified Law as it was written by the finger of God on stone. (That figure suggests both the accuracy and permanency of the Law.) Now, man had a much more complete expression of the law in the form of the Book of the Covenant and the further elaboration of that law in the books of Moses.

Finally, the law of God is revealed in the teachings of Christ and the apostles. Their words are intended to fix our gaze again on the face of God and to reveal his character and will.

The demands for obedience are no less stringent in the New Testament than in the Old. Christ himself affirmed that those who keep and teach the law will be called great in the kingdom of heaven. Furthermore, he said that unless our righteousness exceeds that of the scribes and Pharisees we will be excluded from the kingdom of heaven. The apostles likewise stressed the absolute necessity of obedience to the standard of the character and will of God. The writings of the apostles are not merely good advice but a revelation of God himself—and that revelation is law.

The New Testament itself then is another expression of the character of God to which we must give heed. Paul's words in 2 Thessalonians 3:6 are convincing that obedience to the apostolic word is not an option for the church. It is clearly the name of the game.

Now keep in mind the special sense in which I am using the term "law." The word, as I define it, is bigger than the Law of Moses. That Law given on Sinai was but one expression of the law of God given to a particular people at a particular time and superseded by a fresh revelation of the character of God in the New Testament. However, what I do want you to see is that the law of God as a comprehensive statement of the character of God, stands at all times and can be seen in all sixty-six books of the Bible, not merely in the Old Testament. Law (the expression of God's character) is the unvarying constant of God's revelation. It can best be summed up in the command to Israel (Lev. 11:44) and affirmed again to the church (1 Pet. 1:15): "Be holy for I am holy."

The problem with the law, of course, is that no one can keep it. One might, at least theoretically, keep the strict and statutory limits of the Mosaic Law, but who can satisfy the ultimate demand of the law which is absolute love? The loftiness of the law only frustrates us. Far from being an inducement to holy living, the presence of the law positively stimulates sin. (I recall a story about a lady who objected to the recitation of the Ten Commandments in church because it "put so many bad ideas in young folks' minds.") The law arouses the very action it is designed to forbid. Paul says that he had no problem with covetousness until the full meaning of the commandment "Thou shalt not covet" came home to him (Rom. 7:7). His awareness of the intent of that commandment stimulated him to increased covetousness. The law taken alone can only frustrate.

Furthermore, the law, be it the Law of Moses or the law of our fraternity, cannot mobilize us, motivate us, or empower us to act. It can only reveal and command. Think for a moment about the event at Sinai. At that time the Law was written on stone or on clay tablets, according to the custom of those days. And yet there was more than mere custom in that procedure, as Paul indicates in 2 Corinthians 3:3. The very thought of stone tablets conveys the idea of rigidity and sterility. Stone tablets can only reveal. They cannot empower. Although Israel assured Moses they would keep the Law (Exod. 19:8), while that very Law was being inscribed on the mountain, they were breaking it at the foot of the mountain. And so Moses broke the tablets. I've often thought he probably felt like breaking them over Aaron's head, since it was his brother-priest Aaron who abetted Israel's idolatry. However, he broke them not merely in anger, but in symbol of the truth that no one can keep the law intact. No one can look at God and successfully emulate him. The problem is not the law, which is good. The problem is us. In the inimitable words of Pogo, "We have met the enemy and he is us!" Thus, the law drives us to the end of ourselves.

Who then can deliver us? (Rom. 7:24) God acting in grace! And grace is the second great theme of the Bible. Grace signifies God acting in two spheres. The first is *forgiveness:* the removal of the tyranny of guilt. The second is *empowerment:* the offer of his infinite resources. Law and grace are not opposing principles but rather are complementary. Law (the revelation of all that God is) drives us to Grace (the provision of all that God is) —for *power* to act in accordance with the law and for unlimited *forgiveness* when we fail to act on the power that we have. Thus, law and grace work hand in hand to accomplish God's best for us. Is that not the force of Paul's argument in Romans 8:1–4? In Romans 7 Paul describes his frustration with law-keeping. He knows the law is "holy and righteous and good" (v. 12), but he cannot measure up to its demands. Every attempt to obey the law results in frustration and defeat (v. 24). However, he is not condemned to a life of servitude to sin (Rom. 8:1), "For the law [principle] of the Spirit of life in Christ Jesus has set you free from the law of sin and death" (Rom. 8:2). The "law of sin and death" is not Moses' Law, but rather it is the principle that "evil is present in me the one who wishes to do good" (v. 21). Now, the principle of life in Christ Jesus has canceled out the guilt and tyranny of sin. Our past failures are forgotten and power for a new life is bestowed. Now the requirements of the Law (Moses' Law) are "fulfilled in us who do not walk according to the flesh" [self-effort] but "according to the Spirit" (i.e., dependence on the indwelling spirit of Christ). Do you see how it works? Law drives us to grace. Paul develops the law-grace parallel similarly in the Book of Galatians.

The Gracious New Covenant

This agreement to be gracious—to provide power and extend forgiveness—is the substance of what the Old and New Testaments both call "the New Covenant." The term first occurs in Jeremiah:

> "Behold, days are coming," declares the Lord, "when I will make a new covenant with the house of Israel and with the house of Judah, not like the covenant which I made with their fathers in the day I took them by the hand to bring them out of the land of Egypt, My covenant which they broke, although I was a husband to them," declares the Lord.
>
> "But this is the covenant which I will make with the house of Israel after those days," declares the Lord: *"I will put My law within them, and on their heart I will*

write it; and I will be their God, and they shall be My people.

"And they shall not teach again, each man his neighbor and each man his brother, saying, 'Know the Lord,' for they shall all know Me, from the least of them to the greatest of them," declares the Lord, "*for I will forgive their iniquity, and their sin I will remember no more*" (Jer. 31:31–34, italics mine).

It is helpful to keep in mind the historical setting for this passage. Jeremiah had ministered faithfully to Judah as a prophet for forty years but with little or no response. We know he often struggled with his emotions during these years, and he may have thought that the lack of response was due to either the weakness of the prophetic word or the impotence of God. On the contrary, God assured him, his (God's) word was quite adequate, and he had been a faithful husband to his people. The problem lay in man himself—his heart was weak—so God would do something new. In verse 22 of this chapter Jeremiah wrote that the Lord was *creating* a new thing on the earth: ". . . A woman will encompass (woo) a man." This is remarkable! Israel (the woman), who had been faithless for so long, would now begin to woo Yahweh (the strong man). Instead of the Lord pursuing Judah, Judah would now pursue him, an unheard-of thing throughout Israel's history.

What would cause such a radical change? It would be something supernatural; something only *God* could do. (The Hebrew verb in verse 22 translated "create" only occurs in the Old Testament with God as the subject.) God would "put his law *within* them" and write it "*on their hearts*" (v. 33). The verb "write" literally means to cut or incise (because all writing originally was cut into clay tablets), so the new heart would bear the ineradicable stamp of God's character. Furthermore, they would have a loving relationship with God based on the fact that their sins were forgiven and forgotten. "All will know me . . . *for* [because] I will forgive their iniquity, and their sin I will remember no more" (v. 34). This forgiveness is inexhaustible, linked with the continuity of the sun and moon and stars and all the created order (vv. 35–37).

The New Covenant, of course, was originally formulated with Israel, and its provisions will yet be fulfilled in real history. Israel will be regathered in her land. Her Messiah will come again and reign over his people. His law will be written in their hearts and their iniquity forgiven. This is a covenant "with the house of Israel" (Jer. 31:33), and the fundamental rule of biblical interpretation insists that we see the promise first against its historical setting. The primary application of this oath is to the nation of Israel.

Second, that the basis of the New Covenant is the cross is clear from Luke 22:20: "And in the same way He took the cup after they had eaten, saying, 'This cup which is poured out for you is [represents] the *new covenant in* [effected by] *My blood*" (cp. Paul's parallel use of this passage in 1 Cor. 11). Christ is the mediator of the New Covenant.

Furthermore, this covenant, though confirmed in a prior case with Israel, is likewise applied to the church. We participate *spiritually* in the provisions of the New Covenant. That is the force of Hebrews 10:15 ff.

> And the Holy Spirit also bears witness to *us*; for after saying, "This is the covenant that I will make with them after those days, says the Lord: I will put My laws upon their heart, And upon their mind I will write

them," He then says, "And their sins and their lawless
deeds I will remember no more."

Because of the remission of sins that will result from the
New Covenant the writer says to the church, "Since therefore, brethren, we have confidence to enter the holy place
by the blood of Jesus, by a new and living way . . ." (v.
19). In other words, he concludes on the basis of the New
Covenant that the church likewise has access to the holy
place. The New Covenant referred to by Jeremiah and
mediated through Christ, then, is the basis for the life we
now have in Christ (cp. Heb. 8:1–13). This seems to me
to be an inescapable conclusion that one would draw from
a careful analysis of Hebrews 8–10. I commend it to you
for further study.

Power and forgiveness, the provisions of grace, are the
provisions of the New Covenant and are promised to both
the old and new communities, Israel and the church. But
is this really a new arrangement, a *new* covenant? Indeed
it is not! Power and forgiveness have always been essential
elements of God's dealings with his people. The Old Testament abounds with illustrations of God's grace. In Deuteronomy 30, Moses refers to God's power this way:

> For this commandment which I command you today
> is not too difficult for you, nor is it out of reach. . . .
> But the word is very near you, in your mouth and *in
> your heart,* that you may observe it" (Deut. 30:11, 14,
> italics mine).

Likewise, forgiveness "according to the riches of his
grace" is revealed in the Old Testament. In Exodus 24,
after the Law had been given and the people vowed undy-
ing fidelity to it, Moses "took the blood and sprinkled it on

the people." Since the application of blood throughout the Old Testament is a picture of forgiveness and cleansing, Moses was signifying by this act that God's people were forgiven even before they had an opportunity to disobey. God, being the utter realist that he is, knew that they would fail in their resolve, but out of his love for them he extended forgiveness *before* their failure.

These two passages are only a small part of a mainstream of truth in both testaments declaring that grace (i.e., power and forgiveness) has always been available to men of faith. Grace did not begin with the Cross. It is an *eternal principle*, based upon the Cross. The Cross was an event that occurred in time, but grace is a principle that is not conditioned or controlled by time.

Why then does Jeremiah refer to this principle as a *new* covenant, as though God is doing something he has not done before? The answer is that the term he uses does not always mean something new in an absolute way, i.e., without precedent. The Hebrew word translated "new" comes from a verb that means "to renew or repair" and is akin to the Hebrew word for month, *chodesh*, signifying a renewed cycle. Every thirty days (since the Jews used a lunar calendar) there was a renewal, a fresh start.

Therefore, the Jeremiah passage refers not to a previously non-existent covenant but rather to a renewal of the covenant arrangement that had governed God's dealings with his own from the beginning of time. God has always dealt with men and women according to the provisions of the New Covenant.

In the New Testament (or Covenant) the Greek term for this arrangement is again, a *renewed* covenant. There are two words for "new" in the Greek language. One word, *neos*, indicates something new in an absolute way—something that has recently come into existence. But the New Testament writers use another term to translate the Hebrew word for "New" Covenant. (Heb. 12:24 is the only exception.) Instead they use the other word, *kainos*. Kainos means fresh or different or better in quality, but not necessarily new in time. The writers, I believe, recognized that the provisions of the New Covenant were not previously (to Jeremiah's time) unknown. The New Covenant, therefore, though it was a fresh setting forth of these themes, was not a completely new statement of them. It was, in fact, a restatement of the basic eternal arrangement for maintaining a living, loving relationship between God and man: "God will be our God and we will be his people." As we cast our lot with him and lay hold of his life, he will increasingly bestow on us his power for obedience and his forgiveness for weakness and failure. He will write his law in our hearts and forgive us our sins and forget our iniquities. These are the terms of the New Covenant, a covenant that is not new but eternal, as the author of Hebrews clearly understood:

> Now the God of peace, who brought up from the dead the great Shepherd of the sheep through the blood of the eternal covenant, *even* Jesus our Lord, equip you in everything good to do His will, working in us that which is pleasing in His sight, through Jesus Christ; to whom *be* the glory forever and ever. Amen (Heb. 13:20, 21).

Since the New Covenant is eternal, we should expect to learn as much about the grace of God in the Old Testament as from the New. And so we shall! In the following chapters we'll take a fresh look at some familiar Old Testament accounts. I believe these passages graphically depict the ongoing operation of the Renewed or Eternal Covenant and will convince you, as they did me, that God is eternally the God of all grace—exchanging man's weakness for his strength; man's sin for his acceptance.

—2—

What's in a Name?

From the beginning God's desire has been to establish a relationship with man based upon trust, and it is out of that relationship that we receive forgiveness and power. The ability to be what God intends us to be does not come from human activity but a divine-human relationship. That relationship, as we have seen, is based on the eternal covenant which God has made with man—a covenant in which God establishes that he will be our God and we will be his people.

As we look at examples of the eternal covenant in the Old Testament, we need to consider first the nature of the one who calls us into relationship with him—a nature revealed in numerous ways in the Bible but perhaps seen most clearly in the *Name*. And we want to look at one man's response to that name.

There are several names ascribed to God in the Old Testament, but only one *Name*. The term *El* or its plural form *Elohim* is frequently ascribed to God and is the generic reference used in the widest possible sense for a god, true or false, or even an image treated as a god. *El* is

used in the Old Testament for both the God of the Hebrews and the high god of the Canaanites. Actually, the
term is more title than name.

A second name frequently used in the Old Testament is
adon, Lord, or *Adonai*, My Lord, a term also used in pagan
religions. In fact, several names of pagan deities are derived
from *Adonai*, e.g., Aton, the Egyptian god; Woden, the
Scandinavian god (from whose name our fourth day of the
week "Woden's day" has come), and the Anatolian or
Greek god Adonis.

There is a third name, which as far as we know was unknown in the pagan ancient world. It is The *Name*—the
Ineffable Tetragrammaton (the unutterable four-letter
word) as it has been called—revealed to Israel by God
himself. It was unuttered by the Israelites, a fact that led
to the loss of the actual pronunciation of the name. By
analogy with other Hebrew forms, however, scholars have
determined that the name was probably originally pronounced Yahweh. This is the *Name*—the unique name of
the covenant God of Israel. This name, as none other,
reveals the essential nature of God. The revelation of the
meaning of that name, and with that revelation a new insight into the character of God, is given in the account of
the call of Moses in Exodus 3.

Moses' life can be divided into three distinct periods of
forty years each. For forty years he was tutored in the
Egyptian court by their scribes, perhaps destined in their
eyes for a military career. Josephus, the Jewish historian,
records an uncertain tradition concerning Moses' leadership in a battle between the Egyptians and the Ethiopians.
According to Josephus, Moses was commander of the
Egyptian forces that conquered Saba, the royal city of
Ethiopia, and subsequently married Tharbis, the daughter

of the Ethiopian king. (Josephus, *Antiquities of the Jews*, X, 1, 2). We have no way of knowing, of course, whether this tradition is reliable. However, there is strong biblical and extra-biblical evidence that Moses grew up under the protection of the Egyptian court and thus must have received training commensurate with that position. From any human point of view he was eminently qualified to lead the Hebrews out of Egypt and into Canaan. The second period of forty years was spent in the wilderness of Sinai herding the flocks of Reuel, his father-in-law. The third period of Moses' life is the forty years of wandering in Sinai as the leader of God's people.

The second forty-year-period of Moses' life is introduced by an incident described in Exodus 2:11–15:

> Now it came about in those days, when Moses had grown up, that he went out to his brethren and looked on their hard labors; and he saw an Egyptian beating a Hebrew, one of his brethren. So he looked this way and that, and when he saw there was no one *around*, he struck down the Egyptian and hid him in the sand. And he went out the next day, and behold, two Hebrews were fighting with each other; and he said to the offender, "Why are you striking your companion?" But he said, "Who made you a prince or a judge over us? Are you intending to kill me, as you killed the Egyptian?" Then Moses was afraid, and said, "Surely the matter has become known." When Pharaoh heard of this matter, he tried to kill Moses. But Moses fled from the presence of Pharaoh and settled in the land of Midian; and he sat down by a well.

What a disastrous experience! God's man laid aside. The redemption of God's people delayed for forty years. Disastrous indeed from a merely human point of view, but all part of the divine program to prepare the man Moses to do things God's way.

One can't fault Moses' motives. He saw an Egyptian strike one of his people (Exod. 2:11). He had a heart for his oppressed brethren, the Hebrews. He identified with them though he had not suffered as they had. And so he acted on behalf of his people. He slew the Egyptian and hid his body in the sand. Unfortunately, in his haste, he must have left some portion of the poor fellow's anatomy exposed because his deed became common knowledge among the Israelites and he was forced to flee for his life.

Have you ever had the experience of wanting desperately to do the right thing—giving it your best effort—and ruining everything? That was Moses—the consecrated blunderer. His superior intellect and training had failed him. He had set back God's program forty years. I can identify with Moses! How often have I (to quote Winston Churchill) wrested defeat from the jaws of victory. How frequently have I rallied forth, strong in the flesh, to do some good and noble thing only to discover that I have become the enemy of God.

I recall hearing some years ago of a man who went to visit a friend who was in a hospital recovering from a mild heart attack. He stood for some time beside the bed ministering to his friend as best he could since the man was still under an oxygen tent and communication was difficult. As they talked, this helpful servant saw his friend become somewhat distressed and appear to be blacking out. But before he passed out, the poor man managed to gasp, "Please, get your foot off the hose." Alas, he only wanted to help. Likewise, Moses merely wanted to help, but he added to the distress of his people. They were relieved when he fled from Egypt. Now God has forty years to get his man ready.

The rest of Exodus 2 briefly describes Moses' life in Midian where he found a life among some distant relatives of the Hebrews. The Midianites were descendants of Abraham and Keturah. Moses found a wife there and a new vocation—sheepherding. I once was a part-time shepherd. I had a small herd of Shropshire sheep while I was in the 4H Club in high school in Texas. I can say from my own experience that there is no more humiliating activity than tending sheep. They are filthy, malodorous, and unbelievably stupid—insensate, I believe, is the term. My heart goes out to all shepherds. I apologize to those who may be sheep lovers, but those are the facts! And I'm certain Moses' thoughts were no different. Remember, too, that Moses' culture was Egyptian, and it is historical fact that Egyptians had little use for nomadic shepherds or their sheep. Prior to Moses' birth all Egypt had been conquered and ruled for many years by the Hyksos or Shepherd Kings from Syria-Palestine. The Egyptians, thus, had a special antipathy for sheep which Moses must have shared. How degrading for this highly skilled, superbly trained, and intellectually gifted man. And yet this was part of the process God used to strip Moses of all reliance upon self—his training, experience or background.

Meanwhile, back in Egypt:

> Now it came about in the *course* of those many days that the king of Egypt died. And the sons of Israel sighed because of the bondage, and they cried out; and their cry for help because of *their* bondage rose up to God. So God heard their groaning; and God remembered His covenant with Abraham, Isaac, and Jacob.

And God saw the sons of Israel, and God took notice
of them (Exod. 2:23–25).

Now the scene shifts to Moses, herding sheep:

Now Moses was pasturing the flock of Jethro his father-
in-law, the priest of Midian; and he led the flock to the
west side of the wilderness, and came to Horeb, the
mountain of God. And the angel of the Lord appeared
to him in a blazing fire from the midst of a bush; and
he looked, and behold, the bush was burning with fire,
yet the bush was not consumed. So Moses said, "I must
turn aside now, and see this marvelous sight, why the
bush is not burned up." When the Lord saw that he
turned aside to look, God called to him from the midst
of the bush, and said, "Moses, Moses!" And he said,
"Here I am" (Exod. 3:1–4).

What would you say to a bush that spoke to you? Moses,
I'm sure, was nonplussed! He saw a bush—a common, or-
dinary desert acacia—enveloped in flames but not consumed. So Moses thought to himself, "I'll see what sort
of bush this is." And while he was puzzling over this
strange sight, a voice spoke to him from the bush:

Then He said, "Do not come near here; remove your
sandals from your feet, for the place on which you are
standing is holy ground." He said also, "I am the God
of your father, the God of Abraham, the God of Isaac,
and the God of Jacob." Then Moses hid his face, for
he was afraid to look at God. And the Lord said, "I
have surely seen the affliction of My people who are in
Egypt, and have given heed to their cry because of their
taskmasters, for I am aware of their sufferings. So I
have come down to deliver them from the power of the

Egyptians, and to bring them up from the land to a
good and spacious land, to a land flowing with milk
and honey, to the place of the Canaanite and the Hit-
tite and the Amorite and the Perizzite and the Hivite
and the Jebusite. And now, behold, the cry of the sons
of Israel has come to Me; furthermore, I have seen the
oppression with which the Egyptians are oppressing
them. Therefore, come now, and I will send you to
Pharaoh, so that you may bring My people, the sons of
Israel, out of Egypt" (Exod. 3:5–10).

There are two important things to note in this passage.
The first is that the people in bondage in Egypt were God's
people rather than Moses' people. You will recall that
Moses saw an Egyptian beating "one of *his brethren*" and
because they were his brethren he was moved to act. But
they were in reality and foremost God's people. Therefore,
God saw their oppression and God was moved to act.

The second thing to note is that God purposes to act,
but he has determined to do so through Moses. "I have
come down to deliver them . . . I will send you." Now
I'm convinced that if God had issued that challenge forty
years before, Moses would have immediately responded
and taken it up. Certainly his gifts and training qualified
him for that assignment. Now, however, he is a broken
man. He has lost every vestige of confidence in his own
ability.

But Moses said to God, "Who am I, that I should go
to Pharaoh, and that I should bring the sons of Israel
out of Egypt?" (Exod. 3:11).

Moses now has no confidence in himself—he doesn't know
who he is. If he lived today, we would say he was suffering

from an identity crisis. He didn't know what he could do or what he could be counted on to accomplish—he was lost. And that was exactly where God wanted him to be.

There is an incident in one of the Chronicles of Narnia in which Prince Caspian is to become king of Narnia. Aslan is there for the coronation, and he says to Prince Caspian, "Do you feel yourself sufficient to take up the Kingship of Narnia?" And Caspian says, "I—I don't think I do, Sir. I'm only a child." Aslan replies, "Good! If you had felt yourself sufficient, it would have been a proof that you were not" (*Prince Caspian*, C. S. Lewis, p. 200).

Moses had likewise come to recognize his inadequacy. It had taken forty long and bitter years to unlearn what he learned in Egypt, for there he had been taught, as all secular education teaches us, to depend on himself. An Egyptian stela commemorating the victories of the Pharaoh who may have been the contemporary of Moses describes the Pharaoh as a valiant warrior, one who "loved his (own) strength" (Pritchard, *Ancient Near Eastern Texts*, p. 244). Another was interred with his bow "which only he could draw." That was the point of view of the Egyptian court and all secular society of that day and ours, and Moses was well schooled in that philosophy. But now his strength was gone. He had come to the end of himself as God had intended.

God has now made clear his intentions. Moses is to be the deliverer of His people. The issue is crystal clear—"I will send you to Pharaoh so that you may bring my people, the sons of Israel, out of Egypt." And Moses now responds, "Who am I that I should go to Pharaoh?" God answers:

> And He said, "Certainly I will be with you, and this shall be the sign to you that it is I who have sent you:

> when you have brought the people out of Egypt, you
> shall worship God at this mountain" (Exod. 3:12).

Note that God does not tell Moses who he is. He says,
in effect, it doesn't matter who you are or what your assets
are. I'm with you and that's what counts. We're inclined,
unfortunately, to believe that because we have certain
limitations, there are certain things that we cannot do. Or
because we possess certain positive attributes there are
other things that are right up our alley. We evaluate our
assets and liabilities and on the basis of that assessment
qualify or disqualify ourselves for certain types of activities.
But what is God really saying to Moses? Don't count on
yourself. Count on me! Moses could be sure he would be
in way over his head many times, but he would never be
without resources because *Yahweh was with him,* an infinite resource, adequate for every need. The supply would
be equal to the demand.

Now note Moses' second objection:

> Then Moses said to God, "Behold, I am going to the
> sons of Israel, and I shall say to them, 'The God of
> your fathers has sent me to you.' Now they may say to
> me, 'What is His name?' What shall I say to them?"
> (Exod. 3:13).

Moses' first question had to do with his own identity,
"Who am I?" And God answers, "I'll be with you." Moses'
second question, understandably, has to do with God's
identity, "Who then are you?"

> And God said to Moses, "I AM WHO I AM"; and He
> said, "Thus you shall say to the sons of Israel, 'I AM
> has sent me to you'" (Exod. 3:14).

This is the great revelation of the meaning of God's name. The name Yahweh was certainly known before this time. Moses' mother Jochebed (Exod. 6:20) bore a name that means in Hebrew "Yahweh is glory." So certainly the name was known. The Bible indicates, in fact, that it was known by the earliest men. What is significant about this account, however, is that it is the first explanation for the meaning of the name. The name means "I AM." Apparently the proper noun Yahweh is based on the Hebrew verb "to be" and in this particular form means "I am." At least that is God's own explanation for the meaning of his name, and it seems best to look no further. What then is the significance of the name? Certainly, as many have observed, it means that God is the eternally self-existent One. The One who *is* (there). I believe, however, that a merely theological explanation of the significance of the name is inadequate in this context. Certainly it would be inadequate for Moses at this point in his life. I believe that the name is explained in order to reveal to Moses that God IS whatever Moses needs him to be at any point in his life. God is saying, "Moses, do you need courage? I AM courage. Do you need poise? I AM poise. Do you need patience? I AM patience. Do you need assurance, joy, presence of mind, wisdom? Then I AM all these things. I AM all you need." What a powerful, motivational idea that is! That ought to move Moses to action.

But notice Moses' third complaint in Exodus 4:1:

> Then Moses answered and said, "What if they will not believe me, or listen to what I say? For they may say, 'The Lord has not appeared to you.'"

Therefore God gives him the signs of authority:

And the Lord said to him, "What is that in your hand?" And he said, "A staff." Then He said, "Throw it on the ground." So he threw it on the ground, and it became a serpent; and Moses fled from it. But the Lord said to Moses, "Stretch out your hand and grasp it by its tail"—so he stretched out his hand and caught it, and it became a staff in his hand—"that they may believe that the Lord, the God of their fathers, the God of Abraham, the God of Isaac, and the God of Jacob, has appeared to you." And the Lord furthermore said to him, "Now put your hand into your bosom." So he put his hand into his bosom, and when he took it out, behold, his hand was leprous like snow. Then He said, "Put your hand into your bosom again." So he put his hand into his bosom again; and when he took it out of his bosom, behold, it was restored like the *rest* of his flesh. "And it shall come about that if they will not believe you or heed the witness of the first sign, they may believe the witness of the last sign. But it shall be that if they will not believe even these two signs or heed what you say, then you shall take some water from the Nile and pour it on the dry ground; and the water which you take from the Nile will become blood on the dry ground" (Exod. 4:1–9).

"Who Am I"

Moses' first problem was one of identity, and God replies, "I'll be with you." His second problem was one of ignorance, "Who are you?" So God revealed himself as the great I AM, the adequate one, the one who is sufficient for every demand. Now Moses' third problem is that of authority. When he returns to the leaders of Israel, he fears they will reject him and repudiate his leadership. He had failed before. What assurance did they have that he was qualified now? In short he felt he lacked the necessary credentials. Have you ever felt that lack?

Now what do these symbols mean? What did they mean to Moses and what do they mean to us? It seems to me that collectively they depict supernatural power to cope with any circumstance. Not one of these actions could be explained as arising from natural causes. They can be explained solely on the basis that God is at work. These actions are miraculous. No amount of training, discipline, education, or effort could accomplish them. The only possible explanation is that God is acting through Moses to do the unexpected and the impossible. Moses' authority, then, would be the authority of faith. The elders of Israel would have to take him seriously because they would see about him an unexplainable power—a power that did not arise from his training or title or personality—but from a relationship of dependence and reliance on the God who IS.

The Pharisees once asked Jesus, "What shall we do, that we may work the works of God?" (John 6:28). Jesus answered: "This is [how you do] the work of God, that you believe [literally, "keep on believing"] in Him whom He has sent" (v. 29). In other words, the only way to do the work of God is to count on the resources of the Son of God. How audacious of any of us to believe that we can do the works of God! Only God can do his works. But he will do them through us as we keep on believing him. Faith, then, is the basis of power—power to do the incredible, the impossible. And that power is the basis of our authority.

Have you ever shrunk from a task because you felt inadequately trained or qualified? Have you ever turned away from a challenge because you felt no one would listen to you or accept your leadership? Sure you have! So have I.

However, when we do so, we indicate that we do not know or understand this principle. God's power *is* available to us and will authenticate us if we believe and act on the knowledge that he is the God who *is*.

Moses has one more problem:

> Then Moses said to the Lord, "Please, Lord, I have never been eloquent, neither recently nor in times past, nor since Thou hast spoken to Thy servant; for I am slow of speech and slow of tongue." [The Hebrew may indicate that he stuttered.] And the Lord said to him, "Who has made man's mouth? Or who makes *him* dumb or deaf, or seeing or blind? Is it not I, the Lord? Now then go, and I, even I will be with your mouth, and teach you what you are to say" (Exod. 4:10–12).

How many national leaders do you know with a speech impediment? Can you picture Moses appearing before Pharaoh in his great palace complex at Thebes and stammering out God's message? What a humiliating handicap! But the Lord replies, "Who made your mouth? Is it not I? So you think I don't know about that limitation? Don't you realize I made you that way?" Again, "I AM [is] with you (v. 11). And I will tell you what to say." Note that God does not say I will tell you *how* to say it. God could not have been less concerned about Moses' delivery! God would, however, dictate the content and supply the power to speak. Moses' impediment was irrelevant!

Years ago a young lady came to talk to me about a physical condition that was a great frustration to her. She was terribly crippled, and I certainly understood her feelings. She had a great desire to be useful to God but felt that her affliction rendered her unacceptable. After all, who would listen to a cripple. This passage came to mind, and as I read it, I inserted in the verse, "Or who made you crippled? Is it not I, the Lord?" And she grasped this great delivering truth. It was not her affliction that made her powerless but her unbelief.

Perhaps you have a similar problem. Maybe you are deaf or blind or crippled—or overweight or bald or too short or too tall or whatever. Most of us have something out of order. Who created that deficiency? Will you exchange your weakness for his power?

Remember the Lord's words to Paul when he had those feelings (2 Cor. 12:7). Paul suffered from a thorn in the flesh. We have no idea what that affliction might have been, but it was some terribly disfiguring, debilitating thing that plagued the apostle throughout much of his ministry. Many times (Paul says at least three times) he besought the Lord to take it away. I'm sure he felt as we feel. Oh, if only I could be free from this limitation, this inhibiting factor, then I could be far more influential and effective. But God said to Paul, "My strength is made perfect in weakness." In other words, weakness is no liability to God or Paul. It doesn't frustrate God. In fact, that weakness becomes the avenue by which God's strength is displayed. Without the weakness there can be no strength. What a strange paradox! But what a release to know that God's strength can only be perfected through my weakness. Therefore, I can say when I am weak—he is strong, therefore I am strong. So Paul responds "I will rejoice in weakness." I will *rejoice* in weakness. Not grin and bear it but actually rejoice in it, because only then can I exchange my weakness for his strength.

Now Moses continues, "Please, Lord, now send the *message* by whomever Thou wilt" (Exod. 4:13). This sounds very pious, but actually this statement is a Hebrew idiom that essentially means, "Send somebody else."

"Then the anger of the Lord burned against Moses" (Exod. 4:14*a*).

Now that's arresting; God wasn't angry when Moses didn't know who he was or when he was ignorant of the character of God or when he was concerned about his own weakness or when he felt he didn't have authority or validity. The only thing that made God angry was when Moses said, "I'm not available, send somebody else." And that is also the only attitude that shuts us off from the power of God. Our ignorance, our feelings of inadequacy, our weakness, our limitations—none of these will disqualify us. The only thing that will keep us from laying hold of the power of God is to say, "I'm not available, thank you, send somebody else." But if we're willing to say, "Lord, send me. I'll trust you and expect you to give the power and authority that I need," then God will use us as a deliverer.

You may be facing an impossible situation at this moment in your life. Jesus said that we can do greater works than he did if we believe him. You may be recovering from some cruel, shattering experience. Perhaps your husband or wife has left you. That is a terrible blow. You feel demoralized and confused. You don't know who you are, or what you can do, or where you can find power to live again. Will you believe God? Will you start trusting and believing and expecting him to work through your life? He will do it; he is the God who is. And he has established an eternal covenant with you to provide power to make you adequate for every demand. Remember Paul's words:

> Not that we are adequate in ourselves to consider anything as *coming* from ourselves, but our adequacy is from God, who also made us adequate . . . (2 Cor. 3:5–6).

—3—

Shekinah

The nation of Israel is unique. In the ninth chapter of Romans Paul enumerates some of the distinctives which set this nation apart from the other nations of earth. One of them is the giving of the Law. Only Israel had a Law given by God through Moses. Others are the worship, the priesthood, the covenants, the promises, the sonship (i.e., the special election of Israel by God) —all of these are unique to Israel. And finally, the Messiah himself came through the Jews.

But in that list of distinctives Paul supplies another which is often overlooked. He says that to Israel is "the glory." He is not referring to the fact that Israel merely had special honor, although that is true. It is *the* glory, a specific glory, which Paul had in mind. The glory he is referring to is the Shekinah glory, the cloud by day and the fiery pillar by night which rested over ancient Israel. This was the symbol of God's presence among them, the visible representation of God's dwelling among his people. No other nation had *"the* glory."

The term "Shekinah" is not a biblical term and thus

does not occur anywhere in the Bible. It is a word the rabbis used after the Old Testament period to refer to "the glory." But it is based on a term which *does* occur in the Old Testament and which means "the dwelling." The Shekinah represents God, dwelling with his people.

For a thousand years Israel enjoyed the presence of God, symbolized by the Shekinah. The cloud appeared initially when Israel was in Egpyt, as they were preparing to go out into the Sinai desert. This was the glory which protected them from the Egyptian army. And it was the glory which led them through the desert to Mount Sinai. The Law was revealed from the cloud as it appeared on Mount Sinai. After the tabernacle was erected, the glory appeared over it and filled it—God "dwelt" between the Cherubim on the mercy seat. The same cloud which led them from Sinai to Kadesh-barena and remained while they wandered for thirty-eight years. Then, as they gathered again, it led them on into the Promised Land.

In Psalm 99 David refers to the fact that Samuel saw the glory of God revealed in the cloud. So the cloud must have remained over the ark during the time it was at Shiloh. Later David brought the ark to Jerusalem. And when Solomon built the temple, the cloud once more filled the temple and was the visible representation of God, dwelling among his people. It must have been awesome in those days to approach the city of Jerusalem and see this great cloud resting on the temple by day, and a great pillar of fire by night. No other nation had the glory.

It was there throughout the period of Israel's apostasy and rejection of the Theocracy until the time of the Babylonian captivity. Ezekiel indicates that the cloud departed prior to that captivity. He saw it lift from its position over the Holy of Holies, linger for a moment over the temple court and then hover over the walls of the city as though reluctant to leave. Finally it moved to the east, to the Mount of Olives where it vanished from sight. The temple was "hichabod." The glory had departed. It is significant that Jesus, after the resurrection traveled this same route with his disciples, ascended from the Mount of Olives and vanished from their sight. Israel's temple was left desolate. The glory had departed.

But Ezekiel further predicts that the glory would return. In the final chapters of that great prophecy the prophet records his vision of a temple which many Christians feel symbolizes the millennial temple. Ezekiel describes (chapter 43) the return of the cloud to that temple. The Glory appears on the Mount of Olives at the point from which it vanished in the 6th century B.C. It descends from the mountain, passes through the Kidron Valley, through the north gate and takes up residence again in the Holy of Holies in the temple. Ezekiel thus sees that the Glory has returned. Israel again possesses her distinctive "Glory." (cp. Zechariah 14: 1–21!)

Isaiah, predicting the same event adds:

> When the Lord has washed away the filth of the daughters of Zion, and purged the bloodshed of Jerusalem from her midst, by the spirit of judgment and the spirit of burning, then the Lord will create over the whole area of Mount Zion and over her assemblies a cloud by day, even smoke, and the brightness of a flaming fire by night; for over all the glory will be a canopy. And there will be a shelter to *give* shade from the heat by day, and refuge and protection from the storm and the rain (Isa. 4:4–6).

Thus the cloud was many things to Israel. It was a resource for every need. It illustrates both for Israel and for us today God's covenant to his people.

There are many facets of the history of the cloud to which we could refer, but there is one which is particularly pertinent to our theme. It is found in Numbers 9. The Book of Numbers is an account of the wilderness wanderings of Israel. Our English title, Numbers, is derived from the two different censuses which were taken. The Hebrew title is "In the Wilderness," and that seems much more appropriate, because Numbers essentially is an account of the events which transpired while the nation of Israel was in the wilderness. The first nine chapters are a description of the preparations the nation of Israel made to enter the land, and these are given in detail.

You have to put yourself in Moses' shoes to see the enormity of his responsibility. According to the first census there were 603,550 fighting men, so assuming that figure there may have been close to two and a half million Israelites, including women and children. Moses had to lead them approximately three hundred miles through a trackless wilderness. None of the people had been there before. He himself had been to Sinai, but he probably had never traveled through the portion of wilderness leading into the Promised Land. This would be somewhat comparable to being asked to lead the entire population of San Francisco and the Peninsula to Los Angeles by way of the Mohave Desert. All of them—men, women, children, aged, infirm, dogs, cats, parakeets, grand pianos and all—would have to be guided through an unknown region. And then when you arrived at Los Angeles, the population of that great city would turn out to offer resistance. That will give you some idea of Moses' task. Would you apply for the job?

How could he carry out a responsibility like this? Only because God had promised to be all that Moses needed, and here that promise is symbolized by the cloud.

Perhaps you stand today where Moses stood; uncertain, shocked by the future. A trackless wilderness stretches ahead of you; obviously you've never been that way before. If you are like me, you have 20/20 hindsight, but your foresight is very poor. Who knows the way through the wilderness? I recall the words of a chorus, "My Lord knows the way through the wilderness; all I have to do is follow." We too have a "cloud."

> Now on the day that the tabernacle was erected the cloud covered the tabernacle, the tent of the testimony, and in the evening it was like the appearance of fire over the tabernacle, until morning. So it was continuously; the cloud would cover it *by day*, and the appearance of fire by night. And whenever the cloud was lifted from over the tent, afterward the sons of Israel would then set out [the word means "break up," i.e., break camp]; and in the place where the cloud settled down [that is the Hebrew word "shakan" from which Shekinah comes], there the sons of Israel would camp. At the command of the Lord [in the margin, the *American Standard Version* has "mouth of the Lord," i.e., God was speaking through the cloud] the sons of Israel would set out, and at the command of the Lord they would camp; as long as the cloud settled over the tabernacle, they remained camped. Even when the cloud lingered over the tabernacle for many days, the sons of Israel would keep the Lord's charge and not set out. [The word here translated "lingered" means "dragged on"; i.e., when it was wearisome for them to remain. The Hebrew word for patience comes from this verb.] If sometimes the cloud remained a few days

over the tabernacle, according to the command of the
Lord they remained camped. Then according to
the command of the Lord they set out. If sometimes
the cloud remained from evening until morning, when
the cloud was lifted in the morning, they would move
out; or *if it remained* in the daytime and at night,
whenever the cloud was lifted, they would set out.
Whether it was two days or a month or a year that the
cloud lingered over the tabernacle, staying above it, the
sons of Israel remained camped and did not set out;
but when it was lifted, they did set out. At the command of the Lord they camped, and at the command
of the Lord they set out; they kept the Lord's charge,
according to the command of the Lord through Moses
(Num. 9:15–23).

This repetition and elaboration of a theme is characteristi-
cally Jewish. Repetition is the Semitic way to underscore
an idea. There is no doubt about what Moses is describing;
Israel followed the cloud explicitly.

Anywhere, Father

It is obvious, certainly, that the cloud could provide no
leadership unless the people were willing to be led. You
will note that the passage does not say the cloud drove
them; it led them. Likewise, we are not driven by the
Spirit; we are led by the Spirit. The foundation for all
leadership from God is a willingness on our part to go
wherever the Lord wants us to go—wherever, and whenever and however. Someone once described to me a truck
they had seen on the streets of Palo Alto. Evidently the
driver was engaged in a hauling service and on the side of
the truck door was a sign which read, "Any load—Any

distance—Any time—Any place." If only that were my response to the Lord. "I'll go anywhere, Lord. Any load, any distance, any time, any place." God cannot provide leadership unless we are willing to give ourselves unreservedly to him—with no secret reservations, no small print, and no hidden clauses. No loopholes! That's basic. Suppose Moses looked out of his tent one morning, saw that the cloud had lifted, but decided that this was such a lovely spot that he didn't want to move. Obviously, the cloud could exert no leadership. I am sure, knowing what we know of God's gracious nature, that the cloud would not have moved on without the nation. But there would have been no progress. Flexibility and freedom (i.e., no roots) are prerequisites to discovering God's best. I have to ask myself, "Am I really willing to go *anywhere, any time* and assume any load?"

A number of years ago when my children were younger, I took one of my sons with me to pick up the babysitter. As we stepped up on the porch, a huge dog leaped at us. I didn't see him attack, but my son, who incidentally had on short pants, did, and as the dog lunged for his leg, Brian leaped across the porch into my arms and then scrambled up onto my shoulders. The dog started gnawing on my leg, and the next few moments were memorable as I helplessly danced around on one leg trying to kick the dog and protect Brian. After long minutes the owner appeared and dragged the dog off, but needless to say, for awhile things were pretty hairy! A few minutes later, as I was limping out to the car, Brian looked up at me with obvious pride and said, "Daddy, I'll go anywhere with you!" His confidence was misplaced, I have no doubt. But so many times it has occurred to me that this ought to be my response to my

Heavenly Father, "Father, I'll go anywhere." When we say, "I'll go anywhere . . . *but* . . ." we tie God's hands. He cannot lead when we place a restriction on his leadership. Our Lord knows the way through the wilderness. All we have to do is follow.

The second observation I would make is that the cloud was very conspicuous. Everyone could see it from miles away. It was not a vaporous wisp of cloud which could vanish in a puff of wind or be confused with another passing cloud. It was a conspicuous, obvious phenomenon. It could not be missed. There was *no way* the nation of Israel could miss the plan of God and get lost in the wilderness (unless they wanted to).

God is not playing games with us. He wants us to know his will. *He* wants us to know it more than *we* want to know it! And if we want to know his will, we cannot miss it. Do you believe that? The only people who miss God's will are those who do not want it.

That ought to set us free to live with abandonment. We can rise in the morning and say, "Lord, whatever . . ." and know that God is going to lead us through the day and that his leadership is going to be very clear and precise; we cannot miss it. God is not going to lead us down some blind canyon or over a precipice and then say, "Aha! I fooled you! Your whole life is ruined because you weren't paying attention." How foolish! How alien to the character of God. God has committed his entire being to us. He is our God. We are his people. He will never willfully confuse or deceive us. Confusion and turmoil are Satan's tactics, not God's. If you want God's will, he will disclose it. But, that, of course, is the rub. Do you want it? Some people never find God's will for the same reason that burglars never find policemen—alas, they aren't looking!

Foolish to the World

A third observation I want to make is that it is highly unorthodox to follow a cloud. Individuals follow investment counselors, psychiatrists, horoscopes, and palm readers (not that I classify all these occupations together). But follow a cloud! It simply isn't done. At least no one with any sense does it. If you follow a cloud, expect your friends to question your sanity. Secular man simply cannot understand. Don't expect him to. It is a most impractical way to live. But then, of course, faith always appears impractical. So don't be surprised when people think you've taken leave of your senses. You're in good company. Remember, they thought Jesus was crazy! Why should they think any better of you?

There is a fourth principle we can draw from this passage. Admittedly, it's only inferential, but I believe that frequently the cloud settled down in conditions that were less than ideal. Certainly, the accounts in Exodus and Numbers describe some locations that were difficult in the extreme. That, too, is true to our experience.

God will lead you into situations which are not necessarily of your choosing. There may be hardship and pressure and distress, and God's will for you may be to linger, because *he* is lingering there. And you must accept his will. It is all part of the process by which God is working out his purpose in your life.

Perhaps you have had a very active life and ministry, and now God has set you aside. He may linger there for awhile, for God wants you to learn lessons which can be learned only there. Perhaps you are a mother who has been actively engaged in some service or project and an infant has come into your home, and you are now tied to home and child.

You have to linger there, for that is God's will. That is why Paul says, "In everything give thanks; for *this is God's will for you* in Christ Jesus." That situation you find yourself in is the place where God wants you to remain. It may not be what you would choose, but it is what God has chosen for you.

To Make Us Like Christ

Then I see a fifth principle in this passage. God had a goal in mind when he led them by the cloud. The goal was the Promised Land, the land which God had promised to Abraham and Isaac and Jacob. God was committed to leading the people from Sinai into the land of Canaan. That was the promise and the goal. That is why sometimes the cloud lingered in spots which were less than desirable; that was part of the process of getting from Sinai to Canaan. It was the only way to get there; there was no other route. That explains why God may take us through circumstances which are extremely difficult. The goal that God is working out in our lives is to make us Christ-like, not merely comfortable.

The cloud never wandered. The people wandered, but it appears to me that the cloud did not wander—the cloud remained at Kadesh. The people broke up into nomadic bands and wandered throughout the wilderness. When the thirty-eight years were ended and they came back to Kadesh, the cloud was still there, waiting to take them into the land. God does not wander, does not veer from the path. He has a goal in mind for your life and for mine, and he is going to take us there, though the process itself may be difficult. That is why Paul says, "All things work together for good to those who love God, who are called according to his purpose." And *the* good, in that context, is conformity to Christ—glorification. This is why he can say that everything works to accomplish this goal. So wherever God takes you and no matter what pressures you experience, *know* that the Lord has in mind a goal; he is leading you toward the promise which is the working out in your life of all God's desire for you—conformity to his Son; ". . . He who began a good work in you will perfect it until the day of Christ Jesus" (Phil. 1:6).

God led Israel through a cloud. And he is leading us today, but not through a cloud. The visible representation of the glory, the cloud and the fire of that time, is reproduced in our lives in the person of Jesus Christ who indwells us. He is the glory; we are the sanctuary. He indwells us. The Shekinah is here. And he has promised to provide for us the same leadership that he provided for ancient Israel. Proverbs 3:5–6 says,

> Trust in the Lord with all your heart, And do not lean on your own understanding. In all your ways acknowledge Him, And He will make your paths straight [or, "He shall direct your paths"].

That is the promise—as good as the character of God. "He shall direct your paths." Do you want his path? It all begins with that ultimate act of submission: "Lord I'll go with you—any load, any distance, any place, any time." If you want God's plan, you will never miss it. Most of God's plan is revealed in the Bible. The rest he will unfold as you need to know it through the inner witness of the Spirit of God, that persistent voice within saying, "This is the way. Walk in it" (Isa. 30:21). Don't give heed to hot and cold flashes and feelings that come and go. But those thoughts that grow in intensity and are confirmed by the counsel of mature, Godly members of the Body of Christ are reliable. And you should know that if you want God's will he will see to it that you will not pursue any activity that will ultimately frustrate that will. His aim is conformation to the will and character of Jesus Christ. And his aim is unerring!

"Trust in the Lord with all your heart, and do not lean on your own understanding. In all your ways acknowledge Him, And He *will* make your paths straight." We are like Israel, standing on the verge of the wilderness. "My Lord knows the way through the wilderness; all we have to do is follow."

—4—

Saul: Election and Deflection

One highly motivational aspect of New Covenant truth is the symbol of kingship in the Old Testament. I believe the concept of the theocratic kingdom or God-governed monarchy is intended to be symbolic of our right as Christians to "reign in life." Romans 5:17 states that ". . . those who receive the abundance of grace and of the gift of righteousness will *reign in life* through the One, Jesus Christ" (italics mine). Again Paul writes that sin "shall not be master over you" (Rom. 6:14). Putting those two verses from Romans together leads me to the conclusion that God wants us to reign as kings over our kingdom—our environment and everything in it. In other words, we are to be masters of all we survey, monarchs in our realm, unconquered and unconquerable—truly a noble perspective on life! And I believe that the Old Testament concept of kingship graphically illustrates that truth.

First, let's trace the steps that led to the establishment of the Hebrew monarchy. God first called Abraham from Ur of the Chaldees and gave him the promise that he would make of him a great nation and from among his descendants kings would rise (Gen. 17:6). This promise was fulfilled in part some 600 years later when Israel came out of Egypt a *nation* under God. In Egypt they were an aggregation of slaves. When they crossed the Red Sea, they became a congregation—a nation united under Moses' leadership.

At Sinai they were given the constitution for the newly emerging nation—the Law, Statutes, and Judgments. Then under Moses' leadership they twice traveled to the borders of Canaan. Once they turned back in unbelief; the second time they entered and conquered. The conquest of Canaan gave them their land. Now they were truly a nation, united under the leadership of Joshua, with a constitution and a homeland. Yet one thing was lacking; there was no king in Israel. And that single fact is the resounding theme of the Book of Judges: ". . . there was no king in Israel; every man did what was right in his own eyes" (Jud. 17:6; 18:1; 19:1; 21:25). God did raise up charismatic leaders —the judges—"saviors" who delivered certain tribes of Israel during this dark period, but there was no overall national leadership and the nation foundered. "There was no king in Israel; every man did that which was right in his own eyes." (By the way, it is interesting to note how many *foreign* kings are referred to in the Book of Judges, underscoring by contrast Israel's deficiency.)

Samuel was the last judge of this period, and his tenure marks the transition between the period of the judges and the monarchy. Samuel was both the last judge and the first "kingmaker" of Israel. The appointment of the first king came about this way:

> And it came about when Samuel was old that he ap-
> pointed his sons judges over Israel. Now the name of

his first-born son was Joel, and the name of his second,
Abijah; *they* were judging in Beersheba. His sons,
however, did not walk in his ways, but turned aside
after dishonest gain and took bribes and perverted justice (1 Sam. 8:1–3).

The nation of Israel could not find one thing in Samuel's
life which they could reproach. He was an honest, God-
loving, God-fearing judge. And yet his children went
spiritually astray. We don't know why; they just did. God
never rebuked Samuel for this. Eli, his predecessor, whose
children were also corrupt, was judged because he did not
deal with the sins of his children. But that was not true of
Samuel. As far as we know, Samuel did all he could, and
yet his children turned away from God.

Samuel appointed them as judges, which appointment
they shortly corrupted. So Samuel sent them down to the
south, to Beersheba in the Negeb where they were out of
the way. But Israel knew that at Samuel's death his sons
would succeed him, and the people feared that prospect.
At this same time the Philistines were threatening; the Ammonites (distant relatives who lived across their eastern
border) were ready to invade, and they knew they needed
a strong hand at the tiller.

Then all the elders of Israel gathered together and
came to Samuel at Ramah; and they said to him,
"Behold, you have grown old, and your sons do not
walk in your ways. Now appoint a king for us to judge
us like all the nations." But the thing was displeasing
in the sight of Samuel when they said, "Give us a king
to judge us." And Samuel prayed to the Lord. And the
Lord said to Samuel, "Listen to the voice of the people
in regard to all that they say to you, for they have not

rejected you, but they have rejected Me from being king over them. Like all the deeds which they have done since the day that I brought them up from Egypt even to this day—in that they have forsaken Me and served other gods—so they are doing to you also. Now then, listen to their voice; however, you shall solemnly warn them and tell them of the procedure of the king who will reign over them" (1 Sam. 8:4–9).

You Shall Have No Other Gods

If you read only this passage, it would appear that the nation was wrong to request a king. But such is not the case. God had in fact anticipated their need for a monarch and made provision in the Law for the choice of that figure. In Deuteronomy 17 they were given regulations governing the monarchy and the monarch. May I review for you the provisions of that section of the Law? (1) The king was to be one whom God chose. He was to be God's choice—not the people's choice. That choice was signified through the prophets. The prophets were the king-makers, and as you read the Books of Kings, you can distinguish God's choice from the popular choice by whether or not the king was anointed by a prophet. (2) He was not to be a foreigner, but rather "from among your countrymen." In other words, he was to be an Israelite—a brother. (3) He was to be under the authority of the Word of God. He was himself a subject—subject to the law of God. Hammurabi's Code (written some hundreds of years before Moses' code) makes it quite clear that King Hammurabi, the giver of this law, was exempt from its provisions and penalties. But in Israel every king was to "read a copy of the law . . . that he might learn to fear the Lord by carefully observing all the words of this law." Finally, Israel's king was not to multiply horses, wives, or wealth. In other words, he was not to use his position for personal gain and self-aggrandizement. On the contrary, he was to utilize his kingship to serve.

Now these are the divine criteria for selecting a king. It seems obvious, therefore, that the *idea* of a king was not wrong. Moreover, the Book of Judges prepares us for this event by emphasizing their leaderless condition, "There was no king in Israel." Thus the problem was not that Israel wanted a king; it was the nature of their demands that troubled Samuel. They had rejected God as king. It was God's intention to continue the principles of the theocratic kingdom through the monarch. Yahweh would remain the king, but his rule would be mediated through a human king dependent on him for wisdom and authority. It was that concept Israel rejected. They wanted a "king like the other nations"—an absolute monarch invested with final authority in himself. The kings of the other nations of that era almost without exception viewed themselves as incarnate deities. *They* were gods. They were the final and ultimate authority. Israel wanted that manner of king. That's why God said to Samuel, ". . . they have rejected *Me* from being king over them." Therefore, he gave them their desires—a king after their own hearts— Saul the son of Kish. The story of his rise and ruin is given in the remaining chapters of 1 Samuel. And the important thing to note in this tragic tale is that Saul was a king like the gentile kings. While it is true he never claimed to be a god, he did play the part of God throughout his reign. The principle to keep in mind is that man can only reign when God reigns. When he is Lord and men are subject to him, then they reign as kings. But when they reject his sovereignty and declare themselves independent, self-sufficient

agents ("gods"), then they lose their power to rule themselves and their realm. Follow me through this grim account of Saul's decline and fall.

Samuel's story of Saul's life can be divided into three
parts. The first section, 1 Samuel 9–12, deals with his
election to the throne; chapters 13 through 15, his *deflec-
tion* from the course; and chapters 16 through 31, his
rejection by the Lord. At the end of his life Saul's own
commentary on his life was, "I have played the fool." In
biblical terms, a wise man is one who acts according to
God's Word, while a fool is one who rejects the truth.
Saul had a very hopeful beginning, but his own analysis of
his life was that he had played the fool.

A Choice and Handsome Man

Let's look at this first section, the account of Saul's
anointing at Ramah:

> Now there was a man of Benjamin whose name was
> Kish the son of Abiel, the son of Zeror, the son of
> Becorath, the son of Aphiah, the son of a Benjamite,
> a mighty man of valor. And he had a son whose name
> was Saul, a choice and handsome *man*, and there was
> not a more handsome person than he among the sons
> of Israel; from his shoulders and up he was taller than
> any of the people (1 Sam. 9:1–2).

Saul had a number of natural assets which made him
the obvious human choice for king. He was raised in a
proper family. It must have been a godly family—his
name means "asked of God." Presumably he was a son
who was especially desired, requested, and given as a gift
of God. He was an imposing figure, head and shoulders
above his countrymen. He was bright, strong, and coura-

geous. He had all the natural assets befitting a king, and he had a regal bearing which made him the obvious people's choice.

In 1 Samuel 9: 3–14 you have the account of Saul's search for his donkeys. From Gibeah, his father sent him to find his straying donkeys. Saul traveled through the territories of Benjamin and Ephraim with his servant but couldn't find the animals. They eventually ran out of provisions and decided to return home. As they journeyed toward Gibeah, they "happened" to pass by Ramah. Saul mentioned to his servant that a seer lived at Ramah, and they proceeded into the city to find the prophet (who was Samuel), thinking that he might have information about their missing donkeys. But the Lord had preceded Saul:

> Now a day before Saul's coming, the Lord had revealed *this* to Samuel saying, "About this time tomorrow I will send you a man from the land of Benjamin, and you shall anoint him to be prince over My people Israel; and he shall deliver My people from the hand of the Philistines. For I have regarded My people because their cry has come to Me" (1 Sam. 9:15–16).

This was advance notice that Saul was on his way. Samuel now knew whom God had chosen.

> When Samuel saw Saul, the Lord said to him, "Behold, the man of whom I spoke to you! This one shall rule over My people" (1 Sam. 9:17).

Samuel evidently was just as impressed as everyone else by Saul's appearance, because in the original Hebrew it reads, "the Lord *answered* him," presumably in response to a question: "Lord, is this he? This must be he!" And the Lord responded, "This is the man."

Then Saul approached Samuel in the gate, and said, "Please tell me where the seer's house is." And Samuel answered Saul and said, "I am the seer. Go up before me to the high place, for you shall eat with me today; and in the morning I will let you go, and will tell you all that is on your mind. And as for your donkeys which were lost three days ago, do not set your mind on them, for they have been found. And for whom is all that is desirable in Israel? Is it not for you and for all your father's household?" (1 Sam. 9:18–20).

God wanted the very best for Saul, everything that was desirable. I believe Saul, at this point in his life, *did* seek the best. He was concerned about the political and spiritual situation in Israel, and he wanted to do something significant. Samuel tells him that in the morning he would reveal what is in his mind. The account then describes a banquet scene where Saul, Samuel, and thirty leaders of Ramah discuss Israel's deplorable condition. Then through the remainder of the night Saul and Samuel talked on Samuel's rooftop. When morning came,

And they arose early; and it came about at daybreak that Samuel called to Saul on the roof, saying, "Get up, that I may send you away." So Saul arose, and both he and Samuel went out into the street. As they were going down to the edge of the city, Samuel said to Saul, "Say to the servant that he might go ahead of us and pass on, but you remain standing now, that I may proclaim the word of God to you." Then Samuel took the flask of oil, poured it on his head, kissed him and said, "Has not the Lord anointed you a ruler over His inheritance?" (1 Sam. 9:26–10:1).

And so Samuel inaugurates the new king of Israel.

Donkeys, Loaves, and Prophecies

Then Samuel gives Saul three signs which are confirmatory of his anointing:

"When you go from me today, then you will find two men close to Rachel's tomb in the territory of Benjamin at Zelzah; and they will say to you, 'The donkeys which you went to look for have been found. Now behold, your father has ceased to be concerned about the donkeys and is anxious for you, saying, "What shall I do about my son?"' Then you will go on further from there, and you will come as far as the oak of Tabor, and there three men going up to God at Bethel will meet you, one carrying three kids, another carrying three loaves of bread, and another carrying a jug of wine; and they will greet you and give you two *loaves* of bread, which you will accept from their hand. Afterward you will come to the hill of God [The Hebrew says "Gibeah of God." This is Saul's home town.] where the Philistine garrison is [There was a stockade housing a garrison of Philistines in Saul's home town. That stronghold symbolized everything that was hateful to the Israelites—the oppressive presence of their enemies.] and it shall be as soon as you have come there to the city, that you will meet a group of prophets coming down from the high place with harp, tambourine, flute, and a lyre before them, and they will be prophesying. Then the Spirit of the Lord will come upon you mightily, and you shall prophesy with them and be changed into another man. And it shall be when these signs come to you, do for yourself what the occasion requires; for God is with you. And you shall go down before me to Gilgal; and behold, I will come down to you to offer burnt offerings and sacrifice peace offerings. You shall wait seven days until I come to you and show you what you should do."

Then it happened when he turned his back to leave Samuel, God changed his heart; and all those signs came about on that day. When they came to the hill there [Gibeah], behold, a group of prophets met him; and the Spirit of God came upon him mightily, so that he prophesied among them. And it came about, when all who knew him previously saw that he prophesied now with the prophets, that the people said to one another, "What has happened to the son of Kish? Is Saul also among the prophets?" And a man there answered and said, "Now, who is their father?" Therefore it became a proverb: "Is Saul also among the prophets?" (1 Sam. 10:2–12).

The first confirming sign is that he would meet two men who would inform him that the animals had been found. He was anxious and concerned about the donkeys, and this information would set him free from worry and fear.

The second sign was that three men would give him bread and wine. Remember that Saul and his servant had no provisions—not even a loaf of bread to take to the seer at Ramah. So there would be provision to meet their need.

And third, at his home town in the presence of his enemies, he would be changed into another man. He would be endowed with unexplainable power. He would be able to do things for which he was not qualified by his heredity. He would be given a prophetic gift. Saul was not a prophet; he didn't have the credentials of a prophet, and yet he would prophesy.

And everything transpired as Samuel predicted. Saul did meet two men who relieved his mind of concern for the donkeys. Anxiety gave way to peace. He then was given provisions at the oak of Tabor—three men met him there with bread and wine—and finally, when he returned to Gibeah, he began to prophesy with the school of prophets there. So unlikely was this occurrence that it gave rise to a proverbial saying in Israel. When someone did that for which they were not naturally qualified—something clearly supernatural—they would say, "Is Saul (meaning the performer) also among the prophets?"

These three signs, then, were God's pledge to Saul that he could by God's resources fulfill his kingly assignment. Saul was promised peace, provision, and power—three kingly privileges which we likewise share in common with him. God has delivered us from the pesky and worrisome details of life—the trivia that preoccupy us and drain us of time and energy—by granting to us the peace of God. Jesus said, "Peace I leave with you; My peace I give to you . . ." (John 14:27). What a legacy! Second, we are promised daily provision. Paul writes, "And my God shall supply all your needs according to His riches in glory by Christ Jesus" (Phil. 4:19). And third, there is power—power to do the extraordinary, power to act contrary to one's nature, power to face any enemy (even the Philistines in *your* home town)—adequate power. And God says to us as he does to Saul, "Whatever you have to do, do it, and I will be with you."

This solves for us the question of whether or not God wants us to do the extraordinary. *Whatever* you have to do, do it, whether it is a small thing or great—do it—God is with you. Perhaps today some of you will be called upon to appear before heads of state. Do it! God is with you. Others of you will be attacking a sinkful of dirty dishes or tubful of dirty kids. Do it! God is with you. Or perhaps you have to love an unloving husband, wife, mother-in-law, or whomever. Whatever the task, great or small, do it, for God is with you. There is adequacy to meet every demand. God's peace, provision and power are for you. Receive them, thank him for them, act royally. And people will say of you as they did of Saul, "Is ———— also among the prophets?"

This was God's endowment to Saul. But alas, he prostituted his privileges. He "received the grace of God in vain" (2 Cor. 6:1). In 1 Samuel 13 there occurs the first in a series of three incidents that brought about Saul's demise.

The anointing at Ramah had been a semi-private affair between Samuel and Saul, but at Mizpah he was acclaimed king by the nation. After a successful military campaign against the Ammonites, the nation gathered at Gilgal where Saul was enthusiastically crowned king over all Israel. Chapter 13 picks up Saul's career at that point:

> Saul was *forty* years old when he began to reign, and he reigned *thirty-two* years over Israel. Now Saul chose for himself 3,000 men of Israel, of which 2,000 were with Saul in Michmash and in the hill country of Bethel, while 1,000 were with Jonathan at Gibeah of Benjamin. But he sent away the rest of the people, each to his tent. And Jonathan smote the garrison of the Philistines that was in Geba [or Gibeah—Saul's home town], and the Philistines heard of *it*. Then Saul blew the trumpet throughout the land, saying, "Let the Hebrews hear." And all Israel heard the news that Saul had smitten the garrison of the Philistines. The people were then summoned to Saul at Gilgal. Now the Philistines assembled to fight with Israel, 30,000 chariots and 6,000 horsemen, and people like the sand which is on the seashore in abundance; and

they came up and camped in Michmash, east of Beth-
aven. When the men of Israel saw that they were in a
strait (for the people were hard pressed), then the
people hid themselves in caves, in thickets, in cliffs,
in cellars, and in pits. Also *some* of the Hebrews
crossed the Jordan into the land of Gad and Gilead.
But as for Saul, he *was* still in Gilgal, and all the people
followed him trembling (1 Sam. 13:1–7).

What a sad state of affairs! Israel had long been oppressed by the Philistines. These warlike people, unlike the
Canaanites, were outsiders. They hailed originally from the
Aegean Sea. Called the Sea People by their contemporaries, they migrated to Crete and then eventually through
Anatolia (Asia Minor) came to Syria and Palestine where
they established themselves in city-states similar to those
later developed by the Greeks. They were a very advanced
people, skilled in the martial arts.

In Anatolia they had learned iron working and held a
monopoly in this trade. We learn from 1 Samuel 13:19
that the Israelites were dependent on them for iron weapons—a commodity the Philistines no doubt restricted. In
fact, at this time only Saul and Jonathan held iron weapons. The common Israelite militia were armed with pitch-
forks, shovels, ox goads, whatever—not well equipped, one
might say.

Saul's fortress at Gibeah has been excavated; it was a
crude mud fortress about 160 feet square. Certainly not an
imposing command post compared to the great centers of
Philistine population at Gath, Ashkelon, Ekron, Ashdod,
and Gaza. Also in a classic illustration of over-kill, the
Philistines brought 30,000 chariots, 6,000 horsemen, and
more foot soldiers than one could count to fight against
Israel's pitiful 3,000 poorly armed, ill-prepared, morally

dispirited infantry. No wonder the people trembled (1 Sam. 13:7).

Impatient with God

Samuel had told Saul (1 Sam. 10) to go to Gilgal and wait there for instructions. He was to wait because God was Commander-in-chief of Israel, not Saul. Yahweh of Hosts would reveal the strategy and tactics of this campaign. The story unfolds,

> Now he waited seven days, according to the appointed time set by Samuel, but Samuel did not come to Gilgal; and the people were scattering from him. [The number of his troops dwindled from 3,000 to 600.] So Saul said, "Bring to me the burnt offering and the peace offerings." And he offered the burnt offering. And it came about as soon as he finished offering the burnt offering, that behold, Samuel came; and Saul went out to meet him *and* to greet him. But Samuel said, "What have you done?" And Saul said, "Because I saw that the people were scattering from me, and that you did not come within the appointed days, and that the Philistines were assembling at Michmash, therefore I said, 'Now the Philistines will come down against me at Gilgal, and I have not asked the favor of the Lord.' So I forced myself and offered the burnt offering." And Samuel said to Saul, "You have acted foolishly; you have not kept the commandment of the Lord your God, which he commanded you, for now the Lord would have established your kingdom over Israel forever. But now your kingdom shall not endure. The Lord has sought out for Himself a man after His own heart, and the Lord has appointed him as ruler over His people, because you have not kept what the Lord commanded you" (1 Sam. 13:8–14).

This seems like severe discipline for such a seemingly minor infraction of the rules. A forfeit for merely being off-side? The people were scattering, Samuel hadn't arrived within the prescribed time, the Philistines were massing for the attack. *Tempus fugit!* (Or as a friend of mine says, "Tempus fidgets.") You can understand Saul's frame of mind. He had to do something—anything (even if it was wrong). And so he acted impulsively. He intruded into the prophet's office. He arrogated to himself authority that was not his. In short, he made a decision to go it alone—to act apart from God. He had to "help" God get it together. And the consequences were disastrous.

How many of us can identify with Saul? It is so hard to wait. And yet waiting is, for all believers, the name of the game. Time is always an important part of the process. God seldom, if ever, runs according to our timetable. It is through "faith and patience" that we inherit the promises. It is hard to wait—for a marriage partner, for our husband or wife or children to grow up spiritually, for the right vocation or ministry to appear. It's hard to wait. Time hangs heavy on our hands. Therefore, we must, so we think, become God's helpers. We push ahead of God, to our peril and sometimes life-long sorrow.

Abraham is most illustrative of this tendency. Abraham was promised a son. That was the desire of his heart as it is of every man. Yet the promise was delayed. Ten years passed and no son appeared. Besides, Sarah had passed through the menopause. Humanly speaking, there was no chance for her to bear a son. And so Abraham, pressing the well-known panic button, took Sarah's handmaiden as his spouse and by her sired a son, Ishmael. It should be recognized that Abraham was following a well-established social precedent in taking this action. (We know this from contemporary Near East literature.) In his mind he was not doing an immoral thing. His sin lay not in taking Hagar as his wife but in forcing God's program through. He sought a good thing—the seed—yet he did it apart from God. As in Saul's case, he took on himself the responsibility of determining how and when God's will would be performed. He assumed divine prerogatives—to his everlasting sorrow. The son Hagar bore to him, Ishmael, became the father of the Arab nations, Israel's historic nemesis. They remain to this day a reminder of Abraham's untimely action. He reckoned without God. He sought God's will his way and reaped the long-range consequences.

Alas, that frequently is our plight. We, like Saul and Abraham, want God's best, but we want it on our terms. And so our life is characterized by feverish haste—rushing about "doing good," pushing and shoving, acting frenetically and boorishly to get the work of God done—not acting out of faith and rest. The Christian life is, of course, a life of activity. But the attitude that ought to underlie all action is that of hope—emotionally resting in God, relying on his strength, waiting for his timing. That's doing God's will God's way.

Saul not only lost his dominion that day, but his sons also lost out. Saul had no dynasty worth mentioning. The royal line passed from his hands into David's. It was the seed of David that endured until the Messiah came. And the further tragedy of our frenetic attempts to please God is that we likewise rob our descendants of their royal privilege. Like begets like. And if we are characterized by a spirit of wasteful haste, then our spiritual seed will be so inclined. Our service will result in generations of anxiety-prone, uptight, unbelieving believers. Regrettably, our "sons" will never reign.

One final note. After Samuel took away Saul's activity, Saul went back to Gibeah to pout. Some people are never happy unless they are hustling. They are only satisfied when they are in a spiritual lather. Take them out of the thick of things and they, stripped of self-worth, will simply give up. It takes great faith to "do nothing." Will we never learn that truth? The Lord reminds us, as he did the disciples, "Rejoice not that the demons are subject to you. Rejoice that your names are written in heaven" (Luke 10:20). Self-worth grows out of relationship. Our names are recorded in heaven. So relax and enjoy the Lord. You're something special to him at all times—even in times of seeming inactivity.

There Ought (Not) to Be a Law

The fourteenth chapter of 1 Samuel records the second step in Saul's steep decline.

> Now the day came that Jonathan, the son of Saul, said to the young man who was carrying his armor, "Come and let us cross over to the Philistines' garrison that is on yonder side." But he did not tell his father . . . Then Jonathan said to the young man who was carrying his armor, "Come and let us cross over to the garrison of these uncircumcised; perhaps the Lord will work for us, for the Lord is not restrained to save by many or by few" (1 Sam. 14:1, 6).

I suspect that Jonathan was the man of faith in this family. The odds now were 60 to 1. The Philistines had some 36,000 men, and the Israelites had only 600. But that was of no consequence to Jonathan. And when some of the Philistines shouted from their fortress (verse 12), "Come up to us and we will tell you something," Jonathan responded. He and his armor bearer scaled the side of the mountain.

> Then Jonathan climbed up on his hands and feet, with his armor bearer behind him; and they fell before Jonathan, and his armor bearer put some to death after him. And that first slaughter which Jonathan and his armor bearer made was about twenty men within about half a furrow in an acre of land. And there was a trembling in the camp, in the field, and among all the people. Even the garrison and the raiders trembled, and the earth quaked so that it became a great trembling (1 Sam. 14:13–15).

The Philistines turned against one another, and the Hebrew mercenaries who were fighting on the side of the Philistines turned against their lords and began to fight them. The Israelites, in response, poured out of their holes and dens and caves and assailed the Philistines, who were put to flight. There could have been a great victory in Israel that day. Israel could once and for all have driven these aliens from their land. But Saul again enters the picture. Saul calls for Ahaijah the priest and requests direction from him. The priest begins to reveal God's mind, but Saul looks about him, sees the Philistines fleeing, and so restrains the priest. "Withdraw your hand," he says; "I want to hear nothing more from you." He gathers his army and enters the battle, binding them with a vow:

> Now the men of Israel were hard pressed on that day, for Saul had put the people under oath, saying, "Cursed be the man who eats food before evening, and until I have avenged myself on my enemies." So none of the people tasted food (1 Sam. 14:24).

He made them swear that they would not eat that day. And because they took this oath the battle became difficult for them; they became weak and weary.

> But Jonathan had not heard when his father put the people under oath; therefore, he put out the end of the staff that *was* in his hand and dipped it in the honeycomb, and put his hand to his mouth, and his eyes brightened [i.e., he was strengthened]. Then one of the people answered and said, "Your father strictly put the people under oath, saying, 'Cursed be the man who eats food today.'" And the people were weary. Then Jonathan said, "My father has troubled the land. See now, how my eyes have brightened because I tasted a little of this honey. How much more, if only the people had eaten freely today of the spoil of their enemies which they found! For now the slaughter among the Philistines has not been great" (1 Sam. 14:27–30).

We go on to read how they fell upon the flocks the Philistines carried with them to feed the troops and slaughtered the sheep. They were so famished that they ate the sheep with the blood still in the animal and thus transgressed the Law of Moses.

Do you see what was behind Saul's actions in binding the people with this oath? He believed that victory would be achieved by self-discipline. He rejected the word of Ahaijah the prophet and thus rejected the word of God and substituted a policy of harsh disciplinary measures. When the going gets tough, the tough get going. That was Saul's philosophy. However, as the story reveals, that policy was Saul's and Israel's undoing.

Saul was a legalist. Legalism comes in all shapes and

sizes, but Saul certainly represents one form. To impose extra-biblical requirements on yourself or others as a pre-requisite for success is legalism, pure and simple! In other words, if you have some ascetic practice which you believe will result in increased power or favor with God, that's legalism. *Faith*, not asceticism, is the victory that overcomes the world. Now it is true that some self-imposed discipline may increase your faith and thus give success. However, any ascetic practice followed in and for itself can never make you more powerful or favorable to God. He already loves and accepts you. What more can you add to that? All power is available when we believe him. Do we have to wring out of him additional assurances of love and provision by self-imposed disciplines? That may be Hinduism, but it isn't Christianity. God wants to give—has given—will give. Ours is to receive.

Furthermore, ascetic practices, no matter how assiduously performed, will never enable you to conquer the flesh and its products. Paul, in Colossians 2, writes that the decrees, touch not, taste not, handle not, have, to be sure, the appearance of wisdom, but they are of "no value against the indulgence of the flesh." You can vow great vows, pass laws against the flesh, chastize it, baptize it, simonize it, and it will still turn up flesh. There is no law you can trot out that will subdue the flesh. What's more, the whole scheme sooner or later will backfire on you. Not only will it not control or even temper the flesh—it actually stirs up new manifestations of the foul thing. Paul writes (v. 23) that the result is a show of wisdom in "self-made religion." The Greek implies that we begin to "delight in our religion." In other words, we start taking pleasure in our *system* rather than God himself, and our latter end is worse than the former. Pride, after all, is the deadliest sin.

Thus, Paul says that those who advocate such strong medicine are "defrauding you of your prize" (v. 18). The prize being what Paul elsewhere calls our "upward call of God in Christ Jesus" (Phil. 3:14), i.e., our call of God to be ultimately like Jesus Christ. Legalists never win. Asceticism won't do it. And it didn't do it in Israel. Saul's armies, bound by this fiendish oath grew discouraged, retreated while victory was in the making, and fell into great sin.

The third and climactic event in Saul's inglorious career was his encounter with the Amalekites and their king, Agag. The Lord said to Saul:

> "I will punish Amalek *for* what he did to Israel, how he set himself against him on the way while he was coming up from Egypt. Now go and smite Amalek and utterly destroy all that he has, and do not spare him; but put to death both man and woman, child and infant, ox and sheep, camel and donkey" (1 Sam. 15:2-3).

The complete extermination of the Amalekites was Israelite military policy. These savage Bedouins, inhabiting the fringes of the Sinai Peninsula, had treacherously assaulted the rear guard Israelites as they made their way from Egypt to Sinai. With unbelievable violence and cruelty they struck down the stragglers—the aged, infirm, women and children, at the rear of the column. Though they were ancient relatives of Israel (through Esau), they had no mercy on their kinsmen. Therefore, God declared from that day unremitting war against Amalek. "Remember Amalek," much like the Texans' "Remember the Alamo," became their battle cry. The Lord decreed war from "generation to generation" upon Amalek, and their eventual annihilation (cf. Exod. 17:11, Num. 14:43; 24:20; Deut. 25:17). Therefore, Saul was instructed to "strike Amalek and utterly destroy all he has and do not spare him" (Heb. "be compassionate"). Show no mercy. You can read the story of Saul's ineffectual measures for yourself (1 Sam. 15:4–9). Saul spared Agag and the best of the animals, ostensibly for sacrifice, but actually out of selfish interest. Saul spared Agag, not out of humanitarian considerations, I'm certain, but from private ideas of the sort of treatment befitting a king. Again, Saul played God. And God rejected him from being king over Israel (v. 26). I personally do not believe that God rejected Saul's person. He continued to be a recipient of God's love and mercy even during the ensuing dark period of Saul's insanity. But Saul did lose his kingly prerogatives. He lost his authority to rule, and shortly thereafter was replaced by David, the man after God's own heart. Saul ceased to rule because he would not be ruled. Please know that God's authority is not something to be used, but rather submitted to. God will not give his power to anyone. However, he does release power through men and women who will be his subjects. And then we reign. Submission to the King is the basis of authority. Power in this life and the next is not gained by trying harder, trying longer, or trying again. Power grows out of trust. Begin to believe him. Submit to his authority. Rest in his will. That's the way to reign as a king. Again, "our adequacy is from God." That is the message of the New Covenant.

—5—

David and Goliath

A number of years ago a good friend of mine, in telling the story of his conversion, described his unfortunate experiences in Sunday school this way. When he was five, his parents took him to Sunday school and he cut out pictures of David and Goliath. He didn't go back until he was seven. When he did return, he again cut out pictures of David and Goliath! He went back reluctantly when he was nine and, you guessed it, he cut out pictures of David and Goliath. "So," he said, "I cut out!"

That may be your memory of these Old Testament stories; they belong to some bygone Sunday school era, and you have relegated them to the quaint and irrelevant. Yet, these events happened in real history. There *was* a man by the name of Saul; there *were* people called the Israelites; there *were* Philistines. Goliath *was* an actual person. We can take very seriously what the Scriptures say about these incidents, especially when we remember that they happened as examples for us.

Let's look at another example of New Covenant living; this time from the familiar story of David and Goliath.

And specifically how the New Covenant works in terms of those aspects of life that are perpetually intimidating. I'm thinking of bad habits and other "giants" that dominate us. The point of the story: The bigger they are, the harder they fall.

Goliath was a giant and a mercenary employed by the Philistines. The Philistines were themselves a nation to be feared. Remember they were the powerful "Sea People"— remnants of the magnificent Mycenaean civilization of Greece.

They were an impressive group indeed. And they were adept at psychological warfare, having hired some of the giants of Canaan as mercenary shock troops. These giants are variously called in Scripture the Nephilim (fallen ones), the Zamzummim, the Emim (terrors), the Rephaim (ghosts) —names signifying in some way the terror these gigantic figures struck in the hearts of their enemies. Goliath was one of them, as were his four brothers from Gath.

As I have said, these events occurred in real history, but it is their symbolic meaning which is of profound significance to us. The Philistines represent in general the enemies of our souls—anything that impedes our progress as God's people. Goliath illustrates those specific sins which oppress and frustrate us and have to be faced before we can be free to be what God wants us to be.

Giants in Our Lives

We all have giants—no one is excluded. It may be longstanding bitterness or resentment or perhaps a critical spirit, or some distressing, loathsome practice which has conquered you—you've tried desperately to struggle free but long-term victory has eluded you and so you've given up, resigned yourself to defeat.

But Scripture says that God intends you to reign in life. He never intended that anything should oppress and inhibit you. He wants every member of his family to go on to maturity. So when we encounter giants, there must be a way to bring them to their knees. 1 Samuel 17 reveals the way to win. The setting of the story is given in the first three verses:

> Now the Philistines gathered their armies for battle; and they were gathered at Socoh which belongs to Judah, and they camped between Socoh and Azekah, in Ephes-dammim. And Saul and the men of Israel were gathered, and camped in the valley of Elah, and drew up in battle array to encounter the Philistines. And the Philistines stood on the mountain on one side while Israel stood on the mountain on the other side, with the valley between them (1 Sam. 17:1–3).

There are two things to note from this setting. First, the Philistines were trespassers, occupying land which belonged to Judah. God had given the land to the nation of Israel, and the Philistines had no right to trespass. We need to recognize that this is likewise true of all sin. Sin is a trespasser; an alien intruder. It has no right to possess us. Sin may sojourn for a brief period, but the land belongs to God, and it is his intention that sin be driven out.

The second thing to note is that the situation was something of a stalemate, a classic standoff—the Philistines occupied the high ground on one side of the ravine, the Israelites the other side, with the valley between. Both sides were immobilized. And how often this is the way we feel pinned down, immobilized, unable to move, restricted. We can't retreat. We can't advance. We're stalemated. That was Israel's condition. Now enters the villain:

> Then a champion came out from the armies of the Philistines named Goliath, from Gath, whose height was six cubits and a span. [Depending upon the particular cubit used, he was anywhere from nine to ten feet tall.] And *he had* a bronze helmet on his head, and he was clothed with scale armor which weighed five thousand shekels of bronze [about 125 lbs]. He also *had* bronze greaves on his legs and a bronze javelin *slung* between his shoulders. And the shaft of his spear was like a weaver's beam, and the head of his spear *weighed* six hundred shekels of iron [about 15 lbs]; his shield-carrier also walked before him (1 Sam. 17:4–7).

He was a big fellow—not only gigantic, but powerful! Big men are not always strong men, but here is a man who is both large and powerful, indomitable, unconquerable. The result was that he completely demoralized the Israelites. And isn't that frequently our condition? Giants seem absolutely invincible. They challenge us, assail us. We go out to meet them, and we are defeated over and over again until finally we lose the heart to fight. They master us.

A friend told me some months ago about a problem he had with pornography. There was a so-called "adult bookstore" on the way to his job, and as he walked up the street he *could not* avoid going into the store, picking up the magazines, and looking at them. He had no freedom; he *had to go* there; he was tyrannized by these magazines. I suggested what seemed to me the obvious solution—go around the block the other way. He said, "You don't understand; it starts when I get up in the morning. It's not a question of walking by there, it's a question of being driven. I *have* to go." So often this is the way the giants appear in our lives. They are far beyond us in power, completely dominating us. Struggle seems futile, so we run up the white flag.

Choose a Man—Any Man

Now Goliath lays down a challenge:

> And he stood and shouted to the ranks of Israel, and said to them, "Why do you come out to draw up in battle array? Am I not the Philistine and you servants of Saul? Choose a man for yourselves and let him come down to me. If he is able to fight with me and kill me, then we will become your servants; but if I prevail against him and kill him, then you shall become our servants and serve us." Again the Philistine said, "I defy the ranks of Israel this day; give me a man that we may fight together." When Saul and all Israel heard these words of the Philistine, they were dismayed and greatly afraid (1 Sam. 17:8–11).

Israel was stripped of its manhood. There was not a man among them. You can imagine how these words of Goliath must have stung: "You are servants of Saul (and he's no man at all!). Send me a man, any man will do, just send me a man!" But there was not one man among them. That is what giants do to us. They make us feel impotent. We know that we are not destined to exist this way, but we have no freedom to change. We are tyrannized, stripped of our strength and power. That is what had happened to Israel, and it is what happens to us. The issue is clear: either rule or be ruled. There is no middle ground. One cannot make peace with a giant. It is either serve or be served; there can be no truce. The Israelites knew the chips were down, and now an unlikely hero appears: "Now David was the son of the Ephrathite of Bethlehem in Judah, whose name was Jesse . . ." And there follows an account of David's family, then of his journey to the camp bringing supplies to his three older brothers who were in Saul's army.

David is an extraordinary character. It is my opinion that he is the greatest character in Scripture apart from the Lord Jesus himself. It has always been significant to me that the Messiah is called the "son of David." I realize this is because he was of David's dynasty. But there is more involved than merely his regal lineage. David, as perhaps no other figure in the Old Testament, symbolizes the man in Christ, man as God intended men to be.

David had tremendous assets. Imagine an individual with the literary ability of a Shakespeare, the musical ability of a Beethoven, the hand-eye coordination of a Johnny Bench, and an IQ of 150! And the Scriptures describe him as handsome and ruddy and rugged, from his life in the Judean wilderness. He was in every sense a man.

No One to Trust . . . but God

Yet David had a great sorrow in his life. He never directly refers to it—one has to read between the lines—but I am convinced the sorrow was there. David had a tragic childhood. If you try to trace his genealogy, you simply end in confusion. There are older brothers with sons as old as David. And there are daughters who do not seem to belong to the family. It appears that his father had been married a number of times. And it may even be that David was born out of wedlock. He was rejected as a child. If you doubt that, read 1 Samuel 16, the account of David's anointing. Samuel appears at Jesse's house to anoint a king. He calls for the sons of Jesse, and who are presented? The seven older brothers. David is left in the field tending sheep. Samuel has to ask for him, and David's father resists, saying "He is but a youth." In Psalm 27 David says, "For my father and my mother have forsaken me, But the Lord will take me up." And there are other references by which David suggests that his childhood was tragic. He was unloved, scorned, rejected.

Yet that rejection was a gift of God. David learned from his youth to follow the Lord. The Lord became his life! He learned early to draw upon the Lord, to set aside his own assets, and to trust in the living God. By the time David encountered Goliath he had already slain many giants in his life. He had learned the secret of walking in triumph over debilitating and oppressive circumstances.

In 1 Samuel 17:20 and following we have the account of his appearance at the front. I always chuckle when I read verse 20: ". . . And he came to the circle of the camp while the army was going out in battle array shouting the war ˉcry." Israel gathered each morning, rattled their swords, and shouted the war cry—but no one charged! In verse 23 Goliath appears again and repeats the challenge. For forty days he had issued the same challenge, but no one had responded with courage.

Gird Up Your Loins

But this day, David heard; it is different when a man of faith hears:

> When all the men of Israel saw the man, they fled
> from him and were greatly afraid. . . . Then David
> spoke to the men who were standing by him, saying,

> "What will be done for the man who kills this Philis-
> tine, and takes away the reproach from Israel? For who
> is this uncircumcised Philistine, that he should taunt
> the armies of the living God?" (1 Sam. 17:24, 26).

"What right does this Philistine have to hold at bay the
armies of the *living* God?" Do you see what David is saying? He is taking the first step to overthrow a giant—he is
reminding himself of the truth. And that is where we must
begin. You see, the facts are not always as they seem. We
cannot evaluate any situation in terms of what we see.
What is observable *is* real, but it is not the ultimate reality.
Behind what we see is an all-powerful, living God. That is
the reality.

> Now Eliab his oldest brother heard when he spoke to
> the men; and Eliab's anger burned against David and
> he said, "Why have you come down? And with whom
> have you left those few sheep in the wilderness? I know
> your insolence and the wickedness of your heart; for
> you have come down in order to see the battle." But
> David said, "What have I done now? Was it not just a
> question?" (1 Sam. 17:28–29).

Something of David's relationship with his brothers
shows at this point. "What did I do *now?* I merely asked a
question." You, like David, can expect abuse even from
your brothers in Christ when you act in faith. The flesh
never understands faith. Fortunately, however, the word
found its way to Saul's ears. There must have been a spark
of hope in Saul that made him call for David.

> And David said to Saul, "Let no man's heart fail on
> account of him; your servant will go and fight with
> this Philistine." Then Saul said to David, "You are not

able to go against this Philistine to fight with him; for you are *but* a youth while he has been a warrior from his youth." But David said to Saul, "Your servant was tending his father's sheep. When a lion or bear came and took a lamb from the flock, I went out after him and attacked him, and rescued it from his mouth; and when he rose up against me, I seized *him* by his beard and struck him and killed him. Your servant has killed both the lion and the bear; and this uncircumcised Philistine will be like one of them, since he has taunted the armies of the living God." And David said, "The Lord who delivered me from the paw of the lion and from the paw of the bear, He will deliver me from the hand [literally, "the paw"] of this Philistine" (1 Sam. 17:32–37).

"Goliath is like any other animal I've faced in my past. God will deliver me." Do you see what he is doing? He not only reminds himself of the truth, but he reminds himself that God was faithful in the past. What God has promised, he performs. "He has delivered in the past; he'll deliver in the future. He has proven himself to be faithful to his word."

Then Saul clothed David with his garments and put a bronze helmet on his head, and he clothed him with armor. And David girded his sword over his armor and tried to walk, for he had not tested *them*. So David said to Saul, "I cannot go with these, for I have not tested *them*." And David took them off (1 Sam. 17: 38–39).

You could almost expect Saul's response. He could think only in terms of the weapons of the flesh. That is what he was accustomed to, that is what he used when he went into battle, that is what he trusted, that is where his strength lay. But they were not for David. Because he knew that the weapons of his warfare were not carnal, not fleshly, but they were mighty through God unto the pulling down of the strongholds.

Saul's Armor Won't Work

This is the next step we have to take—not only to bring to mind the truth as it is in Jesus, but also to repudiate any temptation to act out of the flesh. Our mind will invariably suggest an alternative to faith—anything but trust God. When we are anxious, we take a tranquilizer. When we are lonely, we call up a computer dating service. Anything but go out armed with the strength of God alone. The next step, then, is to repudiate the flesh. All the mechanical, human ways we have of solving problems simply *do not* work. They never felled a giant. God has another way:

> And he [David] took his stick in his hand and chose for himself five smooth stones from the brook, and put them in the shepherd's bag which he had, even in *his* pouch, and his sling was in his hand; and he approached the Philistine (1 Sam. 17:40).

David and Goliath first verbally spar. David's final word to the Philistine . . .

> "You come to me with a sword, a spear, and a javelin, but I come to you in the name of the Lord of hosts, the God of the armies of Israel, whom you have taunted. This day the Lord will deliver you into my hands, and I will strike you down and remove your head from you." . . . Then it happened when the Philistine rose and came and drew near to meet David,

that David ran quickly toward the battle line to meet
the Philistine. And David put his hand into his bag and
took from it a stone and slung *it*, and struck the Philistine on his forehead. And the stone sank into his forehead so that he fell on his face to the ground (1 Sam.
17:45–46; 48–49).

David's eagerness is impelling. He slung the rock with
all his might through the giant's open visor. Someone has
estimated that these sling stones are hurled with a velocity
of over 200 feet per second. With unerring aim the stone
struck its mark and the giant fell. Note that David ran into
the battle. The final step, thus, is to take initiative against
the giant. Faith is not passive. Faith is aggressive. Take the
initiative. Say no to the thing that controls you. Believe
that obedience is possible and act on the basis of that faith.
Repudiate its dominance in the name of the living God.

By Faith and Patience

You might wonder why David chose five stones. One
would think that faith would lead him to take only one. It
is tempting to say that he did it because Goliath had four
brothers, and David was out to get them all. I am inclined
to think, however, that David realized the giant might not
fall the first time. There might have to be repeated efforts
to bring him down, but he *would* come down. When he
marched out to meet Goliath, David's word was, "The
Lord has already delivered you into my hands." He was
certain of victory. But he knew it might take repeated attempts.

Hebrews 6 tells us it is by faith and *patience* that we inherit the promises. You may be assaulted again and again.
Don't give up. Don't become discouraged and quit. Be

dogged in your faith. In *due season* you will reap if you do not faint.

Let's review the steps: First, remind yourself of the truth as it is revealed in the Word. This means, of course, that we must grow in our knowledge of the Word by reading it, studying it, memorizing it, and meditating on it so we think God's thoughts after him. Thus we can call to mind the truth in time of need. Then renounce those persistent temptations to gird on the armor of the flesh and act out of the old "tried and true" fleshly methods. And finally, go on the offensive. Put to death the evil practice. Say "no" to it. Refuse to capitulate to it. Believe that the Lord will deliver it up into your hands and strike it dead (vv. 45, 46). And never give up. When you fail, act again—"Sin shall not have dominion over you." Through patient application of faith you will receive the promises.

Notice what happened when David so acted:

> And the men of Israel and Judah arose and shouted and pursued the Philistines as far as the entrance to the valley, and to the gates of Ekron. And the slain Philistines lay along the way to Shaaraim, even to Gath and Ekron (1 Sam. 17:52).

They arose as one man and pursued the Philistines and defeated them. Why? Because David's faith galvanized them to action. They believed and conquered. Likewise, our faith working as an irritant and stimulant will arouse others to belief.

Do you see how it works? This is again the New Covenant in action: His power against our giants. This is the strategy for deliverance.

—6—

A Day in the Life of Jehoshaphat

The nation of Israel is one of the oddities of history; there is simply no way to explain the continuance of that nation apart from divine intervention. For more than three thousand years the nation of Israel has endured and, although it has waxed and waned—at times powerful and at times almost disappearing—it still remains. Israel's continuance is linked in the Bible with that of the sun and the moon. As long as there is a sun in the sky and as long as the moon appears, there will be a nation of Israel. If you ever wake up some morning and the sun does not rise, then you can worry about Israel! Until that time, the nation of Israel will endure.

One of the earliest extrabiblical references to Israel is found on an Egyptian monument which dates from the thirteenth century B.C. It was erected by an Egyptian Pharaoh named Merniptah. He conducted a campaign in Syria and Palestine and returned to record his victories on this monument. Among other things he said, "Israel is desolate. There is no seed left to her." Like Mark Twain's statement: The report of Israel's death was highly exaggerated, because Israel is still very much alive! It is ironic that the Egyptians have that monument in the Cairo museum, a reminder that piquant Israel is indeed alive and well. God has guaranteed their continuance.

And so it is with us; because God is faithful, our relationship with him is guaranteed. He has covenanted with us to be our God, and we will be his people. This "new" covenant relationship is based on the understanding that we are inadequate in ourselves but totally adequate in Christ to withstand the severest attack the enemy can mount against that relationship. We have the story of such an attack in 2 Chronicles 20, which further illustrates the eternal covenant of God. The victory recorded there is perhaps the greatest victory in Israel's history. This campaign is used later in Scripture as a symbol of the final battle, Armageddon, on the great Day of the Lord, when the Lord will once for all deliver his people.

The battle occurred during the reign of Jehoshaphat, a relatively obscure king of the southern kingdom of Judah. He was the fourth after Solomon to reign over Judah, and when he came to the throne, he was a young man in his thirties, eager to do well in the eyes of the Lord. Chapter 20 records a day in the life of Jehoshaphat, and the circumstances surrounding that day are given to us in verses 1 and 2:

> Now it came about after this that the sons of Moab and the sons of Ammon, together with some of the Meunites [Edomites, descendants of Esau], came to make war against Jehoshaphat. Then some came and reported to Jehoshaphat, saying, "A great multitude is coming against you from beyond the sea [the Dead Sea], out of Syria and behold, they are in Hazazon-tamar (that is, En-gedi)" (2 Chron. 20:1–2).

The three nations mentioned here were ancient enemies of Israel who lived in Transjordan. They were related to Israel, having descended from the patriarchs. The Ammonites and Moabites were descendants of Lot, Abraham's nephew, and the Edomites were descendants of Esau, Jacob's brother. Although they were ancient relatives of Israel, they had always been hostile and occasionally engaged in border raids, as in this instance.

Everything Was Going So Well!

It is significant that they mounted their attack at a time when Israel was at rest. This was a time of spiritual victory. God had used Jehoshaphat to bring about a great revival in Israel, as recorded in 2 Chronicles 19:

> So Jehoshaphat lived in Jerusalem and went out again among the people from Beer-sheba to the hill country of Ephraim and brought them back to the Lord, the God of their fathers (2 Chron. 19:4).

It was "after this" (20:1) that the Transjordan nations of Ammon and Edom came to make war against Jehoshaphat. This was a daring and unexpected move in which the invaders had to cross the Dead Sea, probably at a ford opposite Masada, and climb one of the difficult but short assents directly into the heart of the Judean hills. Before Israel was aware of their presence they were in position to strike Jerusalem, the capital city.

This assault upon Judah is emblematic of the trying circumstances we occasionally experience—the unexpected death of a friend or loved one, the failure of a marriage relationship, the loss of a job, or perhaps the attack comes in the form of temptation to return to a vice you felt had long since been eradicated from your life. Or maybe it is a period of dryness in your life when your life seems arid, and you feel that God is not listening; he does not hear nor care.

Frequently these attacks come at a time when things are going especially well. Perhaps you have taken some step of commitment to the Lord which was very difficult, but you did it, knowing that was what God wanted. And you feel somehow that thereafter things ought to go well, but they do not. The car breaks down, you lose your job, your children do not respond the right way, and everything begins to fall apart. That is exactly what happened to Jehoshaphat. At the time when he expected to enjoy the fruits of his obedience, a messenger appeared at his house and announced that an invading army was a day's march away, in En-gedi, about fifteen miles from Jerusalem.

> And Jehoshaphat was afraid and turned his attention [or, "set his face"] to seek the Lord; and proclaimed a fast throughout all Judah. So Judah gathered together to seek help from the Lord; they even came from all the cities of Judah to seek the Lord (2 Chron. 20:3-4).

Jehoshaphat's immediate reaction was to be afraid, and who wouldn't be? We know from the account in chapters 18 and 19 that he had a large standing army, but this horde from across the Jordan was even larger. He knew he did not have the resources to meet this attack, and he was frightened.

We need to realize that an initial reaction of fear is not wrong. That was the most reasonable reaction for Jehoshaphat at this point. It is not an initial reaction of fear which matters; it is what we do with that fear. Does it drive you to be irritable, or to get stoned, or to be resentful and rage at God and at those around us, or to withdraw and retreat? We are not accountable for our immediate reactions to these assaults. But we are accountable for what we do after that initial reaction. When Jesus said to the disciples, "Fear not," he used a present tense—"Do not *keep on* fearing." The initial reaction of fear may be the only reasonable reaction for us to have, but where do we go from there? Do we keep on fearing and give way to despair?

Jehoshaphat set his face to seek the Lord, and he proclaimed a fast in Israel. A fast, of course, means denying oneself food for a period of time. It is frequently the practice of God's people in times of stress to give up the necessary requirements of the body in order to attend to the things of the spirit and to set one's thoughts on God. But food does not exhaust the meaning of fasting. It goes much deeper than that. The idea behind fasting is to deny yourself *any* resource other than God himself. Our tendency in times of stress is to start casting about for some tangible, visible asset we can depend on. We check our bank account or some other resource we normally turn to in time of pressure. But not Jehoshaphat. He declared a fast and set his face to seek the Lord.

So the first thing to do when you are afraid is to reject the tendency to count on the tangible and natural and set your face to seek the Lord. Remind yourself that he and he alone is the source of help.

> Then Jehoshaphat stood in the assembly of Judah and Jerusalem, in the house of the Lord before the new court, and he said, "O Lord, the God of our fathers, art Thou not God in the heavens? And art Thou not ruler over all the kingdoms of the nations? Power and

> might are in Thy hand so that no one can stand
> against Thee. Didst Thou not, O our God, drive out
> the inhabitants of this land before Thy people Israel,
> and give it to the descendants of Abraham Thy friend
> forever? And they lived in it, and have built Thee a
> sanctuary there for Thy name, saying, 'Should evil
> come upon us, the sword, or judgment, or pestilence, or
> famine . . .'" (2 Chron. 20:5–9).

Sword, judgment, pestilence, and famine suggest an assortment of assaults that are directed against our peace and security in Christ. So it seems to me. The sword symbolizes those great tragedies that strike us down—the death of a loved one we have always depended upon, or other major catastrophic loss. Judgment may suggest those feelings of guilt and condemnation by which most of us are assailed periodically. In the ancient world a pestilence was a plague that struck either land or people in epidemic proportions and thus represents those wide-ranging and seemingly never-ending mental or physical sieges that so drain us of energy and determination. A famine, of course, represents a period of aridity and spiritual dryness. These attacks come unexpectedly and for no apparent reason. And often they come in waves. How shall we respond? Note Jehoshaphat's reaction:

> "'. . . we will stand before this house and before Thee
> (for Thy name is in this house) and cry to Thee in our
> distress, and Thou wilt hear and deliver *us*.' And now
> behold, the sons of Ammon and Moab and Mount
> Seir, whom Thou didst not let Israel invade, when they
> came out of the land of Egypt (they turned aside
> from them and did not destroy them), behold *how*
> they are rewarding us, by coming to drive us out from

Thy possession which Thou hast given us as an inheritance. O our God, wilt Thou not judge them? For we
are powerless before this great multitude who are coming against us; nor do we know what to do, but our eyes
are on Thee." And all Judah was standing before the
Lord with their infants, their wives, and their children
(2 Chron. 20:9–13).

The next step Jehoshaphat takes is to remind himself
that God is the source of his help. Then, he reminds himself of who God is (shades of Moses!). Notice that twice
he asks the question, "are you not . . ." "Are you not God
in the heavens? And are you not ruler over all the kingdoms
of the nations?" He begins by calling to his mind who the
Lord really is. "Aren't you the God in the heavens? Don't
you reign in the realm of spiritual realities? Aren't you
sovereign? Is your throne threatened? Is it shaky?" Is God
pacing the floor and biting his nails and pulling his hair,
filled with anguish over the state of affairs in his world?

An ancient limerick comes to mind,

> The world had a hopeful beginning
>   But man spoiled his chances through sinning.
> We trust that the story will end to God's glory
>   But at present the other side's winning!

Does that bit of terse verse truly represent the condition of
God's kingdom? Absolutely not! It is true that God is not
necessarily trying to run the world right in all particulars.
He is letting man go and reap the results of their rebellion.
It may appear at times, therefore, that the other side is win-
ning. But God is in control. His rule is not threatened. He
is utterly unruffled, unshaken—absolutely tranquil in his
kingly rule.

Where Are the Waves?

In the Book of Revelation, there is a reference to "a sea of glass" with which the throne of God is surrounded. This untroubled sea is symbolic of the peace which surrounds God. Have you ever seen a sea like glass? That condition occurs infrequently. Usually the sea is troubled and agitated. But a sea without chop, without waves, is a graphic picture of peace and quiet. One time when my family and I were at Lake Tahoe, Joshua, our youngest son, kept asking, "Where are the waves?" It was one of those rare windless days, and that crystal clear mountain lake was like glass. You could see the mountains, trees, and sky reflected as in a mirror, and I thought of that passage in Revelation. It was like the tranquility of God. "Art thou not God in the heavens?"

God is in control of the heavens and the nations of the world—*all* the nations. That means he ruled over the Ammonites and the Moabites and the Edomites, as he rules today in the Middle East and in every troubled nation and location in our world. He rules over our President and his cabinet and others who are associated with him in leadership. He rules over your family and mine, over your circumstances, and your past, present, and future. Whatever your situation is, God rules. He is sovereign. He is not under attack, nor threatened; he is at peace.

Then Jehoshaphat reminds himself not only of who God is, but of what he can do, and has done in the past:

> Didst Thou not, O our God, drive out the inhabitants of this land before Thy people Israel, and give it to the descendants of Abraham Thy friend forever? And they lived in it, and have built Thee a sanctuary there for Thy name . . . (2 Chron. 20:7-8).

He calls to mind the conquest of Canaan and his promise that the land is theirs for eternity. No matter who might try to force them out of the land, the land belonged to them, and God would guarantee them their place. God's mighty deeds in history were undeniable.

Notice that in verse 6, Jehoshaphat says, "Power and might are in Thy hand," and then in verse 12, he says, "We are powerless." Isn't this exactly what Paul says in his explanation of the ministry of the New Covenant in 2 Corinthians? "Not that we are adequate in ourselves . . . but our adequacy is from God" (2 Cor. 3:5). Jehoshaphat understood this, but it is a hard lesson for most of us to learn.

A long time ago, it seems, I went to Highland Park High School in Dallas, Texas. For some reason, the three years I was there we had a disastrous athletic program. The year I was a senior we lost the first six football games of the season, and it did not look as if the rest of the season was going to be any better. I remember attending a pep rally at that time. The cheerleaders were jumping up and down and leading everyone in a yell that went something like this:

> Victory, victory, is our cry;
> V–I–C–T–O–R–Y.
> Can we do it? Well I guess,
> Highland Park High School
> Yes, Yes, Yes!

And I remember that it struck me just how hollow those words were after six losses and not much possibility of improvement. "Can we do it? Well I guess!" It reminds me now of the words of the poem:

> He tackled the thing that couldn't be done
>   With a will he went right to it
> He tackled the thing that couldn't be done . . .
>   And he couldn't do it!

Can I identify with that approach to problems! I venture forth singing fight songs to tackle the impossible. Outside I look bold and assured, but, as a friend of mine says, inside I'm shredded wheat. What fakery. Why don't we admit what we know is true. We are powerless. Power and might are in his hand. All we can do is say, "Lord, I don't have the power. I don't know what to do. I don't know where to go, except to you. And my eyes are on you. I'm going to stand on the truth that you are able to accomplish on my behalf all that you have promised to do."

Go Out and Face Them

Whenever we take that position, God always responds. Someone has said that through the ages, if men needed wisdom, they might have cried out, "William Shakespeare, help me!" and nothing much would have happened. Or if they needed courage, they might cry out, "Billy Budd, help me!" and nothing much would happen. But for nineteen hundred years, whenever men have cried out, "Lord Jesus, help me," something has always happened. And this was true in the life of Israel. Whenever they cried out to the Lord, something happened.

> Then in the midst of the assembly the Spirit of the Lord came upon Jahaziel [Often help comes from the most unlikely quarter. From the midst of the congregation someone began to speak.] the son of Zechariah, the son of Benaiah, the son of Jeiel, the son of Mattaniah, the Levite of the sons of Asaph; and he said,

"Listen, all Judah and the inhabitants of Jerusalem and King Jehoshaphat: thus says the Lord to you, 'Do not fear or be dismayed because of this great multitude, for the battle is not yours but God's. Tomorrow go down against them. Behold, they will come up by the ascent of Ziz, and you will find them at the end of the valley in front of the wilderness of Jeruel [just outside the gates of Jerusalem]. You *need* not fight in this *battle*; station yourselves [the Hebrew says, "Take a stand"], stand and see the salvation of the Lord on your behalf, O Judah and Jerusalem.' Do not fear or be dismayed; tomorrow go out to face them, for the Lord is with you. And Jehoshaphat bowed his head with *his* face to the ground, and all Judah and the inhabitants of Jerusalem fell down before the Lord, worshiping the Lord. And the Levites, from the sons of the Kohathites and of the sons of the Korahites, stood up to praise the Lord God of Israel, with a very loud voice (2 Chron. 20:14–19).

Now they are on top of things because they realize that the demand ultimately rests upon the Lord, and he is adequate to face this circumstance. They do not need to fight; they only need to stand still and God will do battle. But it is obvious that this stand is not merely a physical posture they are to maintain. They are also to go out and face the enemy. Standing is a mental posture. It is a position we take based on our understanding of who God is and what he will do. We stand fast in our mind, but we have to face the opposition whatever it is. It is never God's will for us to run from a difficult circumstance. I know from my own experience that whenever I have done this, sooner or later God has brought me back to face it again. He wants to teach me that I *can* face into any obstacle, any problem, as long as my stance is right, as long as I am standing—mentally and spiritually—on the truth that I know about God.

But this is an attitude which has to be renewed again and again. I cannot once-for-all-time bid my anxiety flee. My experience is that I will resolve the issue many times. Sometimes I will go to bed at night with a quiet and peaceful heart. But when I awaken the next morning—and for a few seconds everything is okay while I try to remember who I am, but by the time I get the alarm turned off—suddenly I am assaulted again by doubt and fear. "How in the world am I going to do this thing today that I dread so much?" And again I am overcome. And this must be what happened to Israel because Jehoshaphat had to remind them again of the basis of victory.

> And they rose early in the morning and went out to the wilderness of Tekoa; and when they went out, Jehoshaphat stood and said, "Listen to me, O Judah and inhabitants of Jerusalem, put your trust in the Lord your God, and you will be established. Put your trust in His prophets and succeed" (2 Chron. 20:20).

Here he equates the word of the prophets with the Word of God. "Put your trust in the Lord—put your trust in his prophets." He is doing what you and I must do every morning and repeatedly during the day: remind ourselves of the truth of God's Word and then take our mental stand on those facts. Because fear will come back again and again, and we have to pause and get our eyes off the circumstances, off the things we would normally rely upon and back on the Lord. We must realize it is from him that we receive our strength. We may have to do this many, many times through the day. But the result is that, having done it, we will stand, and face the thing we dread.

And when he had consulted with the people, he appointed those who sang to the Lord and those who praised *Him* in holy attire, as they went out before the army and said, "Give thanks to the Lord, for His lovingkindness is everlasting" (2 Chron. 20:21).

They began to sing and praise God *and give thanks* for the victory that was already theirs. They were thanking God in advance for the victory over this coalition of nations. And that is the action of faith! In Philippians 4 Paul writes, "Be anxious for nothing, but in everything by prayer and supplication *with thanksgiving* let your requests be made known to God" (italics mine). Lord, I need courage to face this circumstance tomorrow. Thank you that I have it. Lord, I need love to handle this situation tonight. Thank you that I have it. It is walking in the expectation that God will fulfill his promises which is the true expression of faith. "Thank you, God, that you are going to do everything you have promised to do."

Dead on Arrival

Now notice how God brings about the victory for Israel:

And *when* they began singing and praising [and only then], the Lord set ambushes against the sons of Ammon, Moab, and Mount Seir, who had come against Judah; so they were routed. For the sons of Ammon and Moab rose up against the inhabitants of Mount Seir destroying *them* completely, and when they had finished with the inhabitants of Seir, they helped to destroy one another (2 Chron. 20:22–23, italics mine).

Let's put ourselves in Israel's sandals and try to imagine what occurred on the line of march. As they descended through the wilderness of Tekoa, they would occasionally come to a rise from which they could view the Transjordanian armies massed for the attack. Then they would be lost from sight as they dropped into a ravine. Again they would climb another rise and look down the Ascent of Ziz and the enemy would still be approaching. The tension builds! They descend and top another rise. The enemy is still there, advancing steadily in their direction. But the Judeans are singing and praising God. They drop into another valley and approach the final rise—this time with swords drawn—but the enemy has been vanquished! They are dead on arrival! And notice, please, that the enemy forces fell upon one another "*when* they began singing and praising the Lord." The victory is clearly linked with their spirit of praise and thanksgiving that demonstrated that faith.

> When Judah came to the lookout of the wilderness, they looked toward the multitude; and behold, they *were* corpses lying on the ground, and no one had escaped (2 Chron. 20:24).

Has this happened to you lately? Of course it has if you are learning to meet fear with faith. All of us face challenges that far exceed our wherewithal. (One immediately thinks of those moments when one knee said to the other, "Let's shake.") However, despite your fear, or more true to my experience, in the midst of your fear, when you face into the thing you fear and do so with faith and expectancy, frequently the actual encounter with the dreaded thing is almost an anticlimax. It poses no threat at all. It is dead on arrival.

> And when Jehoshaphat and his people came to take their spoil, they found much among them, *including* goods, garments, and valuable things which they took for themselves, more than they could carry. And they were three days taking the spoil because there was so much (2 Chron. 20:25).

Adversity is turned into triumph. They returned with the spoils of war. Is this not what Paul means when he says we are "more than conquerors through him who loved us"? God takes the traumatic, tragic circumstances of our life and turns them to ringing triumph.

> Then on the fourth day they assembled in the valley of Beracah [the Hebrew word which means "blessing"], for there they blessed the Lord. Therefore they have named that place "The Valley of Beracah" until today [the time of the Exile, when this was written. I understand that valley is still called today The Valley of Beracah]. And every man of Judah and Jerusalem returned with Jehoshaphat at their head, returning to Jerusalem with joy, for the Lord had made them to rejoice over their enemies. And they came to Jerusalem with harps, lyres, and trumpets to the house of the Lord. And the dread of God was on all the kingdoms of the lands when they heard that the Lord had fought against the enemies of Israel. So the kingdom of Jehoshaphat was at peace, for his God gave him rest on all sides (2 Chron. 20:26–30).

That will be your experience and mine as we act upon the principles laid out in this passage. When you are assaulted and tempted to give way to fear, remind yourself of the source of your help and deny the inclination to draw on other resources. Call to mind who the Lord is and what he has done in your own history, and, therefore, what he is capable of doing. Take your stand on that fact rather than your feelings. And advance into that dreadful encounter. You will discover to your everlasting delight that God turns adversity into an opportunity for advancement. The thing you feared is rendered impotent. The encounter will go down in your history as the "Valley of Beracah," and your kingdom will be at rest as was Jehoshaphat's. You have nothing to fear but fear; or put more profoundly, to a crow in the know a scarecrow is an invitation to a feast!

The Prophet Joel, in speaking of the second coming of our Lord and the great and climactic deliverance of Israel, his people, calls the place of the final conflict (though the battle takes place far north of Jerusalem) "The Valley of Jehoshaphat." Thus, this battle, recorded in 2 Chronicles 20, is emblematic of all God's victories and more especially the final and unalterable conquest of the enemies of God's people. Every valley can be for us the Valley of Jehoshaphat. The name, Jehoshaphat, means "Yahweh judges." May God judge all your enemies.

—7—

Manasseh: The Prodigal King

If you are like me, I am sure that you have things in your life you would like to forget, memories which come back to haunt you from time to time. Many things in our past make us feel guilty, defiled, and unacceptable. Time and again I have had to turn to the Scriptures to find release from a sense of guilt about my past, and I have discovered that there is encouragement and liberating instruction there. The story of Manasseh has ministered to me in this respect, and it illustrates clearly the principle of the New Covenant: that God has forgotten our sins and iniquities.

> So Hezekiah slept with his fathers, and Manasseh his son became king in his place. Manasseh was twelve years old when he became king, and he reigned fifty-five years in Jerusalem; and his mother's name was Hephzibah (2 Kings 20:21; 21:1).

Manasseh was the son of Hezekiah, who was one of the few kings Judah called "good." Many were not. Hezekiah was responsible for a spiritual revival during his reign which swept the entire nation. He did away with the idolatry that his father, Ahaz, had established and purged the nation of apostasy. We know that he was helped in his reign by the prophetic ministry of Isaiah and Micah. There were at least two invasions of Judah during this time by Sennacherib, the king of Assyria. On both of these occasions the Lord protected Jerusalem. Although almost all of the land of Judah was devastated by the Assyrians, the capital city was preserved. Isaiah described Jerusalem as a caretaker's hut in the midst of the cucumber field, and Sennacherib, in his own annals, says he "shut up Hezekiah like a bird in a cage." All the fortified cities had been destroyed, but Jerusalem was left. It was Hezekiah's wise leadership which made possible the preservation of the city and its people. He was a powerful spiritual force in Judah.

More Evil

Manasseh came to the throne when he was twelve years old and reigned for about ten years as co-regent with his father. When Manasseh was twenty-two, his father died, and the young man took over the reins of government. Keep in mind that Manasseh had a godly father, he lived in a time of spiritual vitality and prosperity, and he had the words of the prophets Isaiah and Micah ringing in his ears. He had seen the Lord deliver Jerusalem in a very miraculous way when it was under siege by the Assyrians. And yet,

> . . . he did evil in the sight of the Lord, according to the abominations of the nations whom the Lord dispossessed before the sons of Israel (2 Kings 21:2).

The nations referred to here are the terribly decadent Canaanite nations which were expelled by Joshua and the twelve tribes when they conquered the land. And yet the Scriptures say that Manasseh *outdid* the Canaanite nations in his wickedness. Note verse 9: ". . . Manasseh seduced them to do evil *more* than the nations whom the Lord destroyed before the sons of Israel"; and verse 11: ". . . having done wickedly *more* than all the Amorites did who were before him . . ." He was more wicked than the nations that God drove from the land when the Israelites took possession of it.

Verses 3 through 9 explain the abominations that Manasseh introduced. First: ". . . he rebuilt the high places which Hezekiah his father had destroyed . . ."

The father of Hezekiah was Ahaz. Ahaz had established "high places," groves on the top of hills throughout Judah where the Asherah were worshiped. Hezekiah had destroyed them, but Manasseh built them again: ". . . and he erected altars for Baal . . ." (Baal was the chief Canaanite deity) ". . . and made an Asherah, as Ahab king of Israel had done . . ." Asherah was a female deity, the consort of Baal and the goddess of sex and fertility. Many scholars believe that the monuments built in her honor were phallic symbols.

Manasseh reintroduced this Canaanite sex cult into the nation of Israel: ". . . and worshiped all the host of heaven and served them." He worshiped the sun, the moon, the planets, and the stars, and practiced astrology.

> And he built altars in the house of the Lord, of which the Lord had said, "In Jerusalem I will put My name." For he built altars for all the host of heaven in the two courts of the house of the Lord.

He placed altars to foreign gods in the temple itself—in the outer court and in the holy place where the priests worshiped.

"And he made his son pass through the fire . . ." He sacrificed his own son to Molech, the god of the Amorites. And he ". . . practised witchcraft and used divination, and dealt with mediums and spiritists." The Hebrew is much stronger here than the English translation. He actually placed mediums and spiritists and those who dealt in the occult in positions of leadership.

> Then [as though this were not enough] he set the carved image of Asherah that he had made, in the house of which the Lord said to David and to his son Solomon, "In this house and in Jerusalem, which I have chosen from all the tribes of Israel, I will put My name forever. And I will not make the feet of Israel wander any more from the land which I gave their fathers, if only they will observe to do according to all the law that My servant Moses commanded them."

He took these phallic objects, dedicated to everything immoral and obscene, and put them in the Holy of Holies, in the place where the Spirit of God dwelt.

Now, it is significant that nowhere in this account is there any mention of the worship of Yahweh. Manasseh selected his pantheon from all the cultures surrounding Israel—from the Amorites, the Canaanites, the Philistines, the Phoenicians—but not one reference is made to the worship of the God of Israel. In summary, "Manasseh seduced them to do evil more than the nations whom the Lord destroyed before the sons of Israel."

Hear the Lord's response:

> Now the Lord spoke through His servants the proph-
> ets, saying, "Because Manasseh king of Judah has done
> these abominations, having done wickedly more than
> all the Amorites did who *were* before him, and has also
> made Judah sin with his idols; therefore thus says the
> Lord, the God of Israel, 'Behold, I am bringing *such*
> calamity on Jerusalem and Judah, that whoever hears
> of it, both his ears shall tingle. And I will stretch over
> Jerusalem the line of Samaria and the plummet of the
> house of Ahab . . .' "

"As a surveyor would take a transit and level out a
place on which to build," the Lord said, "that is what I am
going to do to Jerusalem. I will level it as I leveled Samaria
and the house of Ahab. The extermination experienced
by the northern kingdom of Israel and the house of
Ahab is the measure of the extermination of Jerusalem.
. . . and I will wipe Jerusalem as one wipes a dish, wiping
it and turning it upside down." What a vivid picture!
There will not be one trace left—total extermination.

> " 'And I will abandon the remnant of My inheritance
> and deliver them into the hand of their enemies, and
> have been provoking Me to anger, since the day their
> enemies; because they have done evil in My sight, and
> have been provoking Me to anger, since the day their
> fathers came from Egypt, even to this day' " (2 Kings
> 21:10–15).

There are two things I want you to note. First, Manasseh
was obviously a wicked man. He was perhaps the most
wicked king that ever reigned over Judah. And yet who of

us can sit in judgment upon him? We can all look back into our lives and see that we have done the same things! It is only a question of degree. We may not have worshiped Baal and Asherah per se, but we have erected other idols in our spirit. We worship our vocation, or the pursuit of a degree, or our house, or a man or woman. Or we may quite literally set up a phallic symbol in our own spirits, the Holy of Holies of man, and worship sex. We are as culpable as Manasseh, just as worthy of judgment. Let's face that fact!

God Loved Manasseh

The second thing I want you to observe is the procedure the Lord undertakes to reclaim his man. God loved Manasseh, and because he loved him, he would not allow him to continue in rebellion. First he spoke quietly out of Manasseh's memory (v. 4). As Manasseh began to indulge in these idolatrous practices God said, "Manasseh, Jerusalem is where I have placed my name." That is, "Jerusalem is my possession. You shall not have any other gods before me there." And then when Manasseh didn't listen, God's voice from the past came with greater clarity and insistence (vv. 7, 8). He reminded him of his promises, both positive and negative—promises of blessing if Manasseh would obey and of a great judgment if he did not. And finally, God thundered at him through the prophets (v. 10) so that everywhere Manasseh turned he was faced with the voice of God. He could not avoid it.

Have you had that experience? Have you ever been hounded by his relentless love? First, the Lord will speak to us in a gentle, quiet, gracious way. He reminds us that we belong to him. If we don't listen, he speaks with greater clarity through his Word and through his Spirit, witnessing to our spirit. And then if we still won't listen, he sur-

rounds us with many witnesses to the truth, so that everywhere we turn we hear the voice of God. We can't get
away. At times when I have been in headlong flight from
the Lord, even when I think I've gotten away scot-free, I
hear him say, "Here I am." I turn on the radio and, there
he is! I feel like David: "If I made my bed in hell" I
would hear his voice; "Here I am!"

I had an appointment with a student at Stanford Uni-
versity one day. I waited for him in front of the chapel, but
he was late. Another student was sitting on a bench nearby,
so I sat down and started to chat with him. When I discovered that he was born in China, I asked him a bit about
his past. The Lord opened an opportunity to share the
gospel with him and to tell him of the Lord's love for him.
But as I began to speak, he got very angry and jumped to
his feet! His reaction was so unusually adverse that I was
quite surprised. I asked him what was wrong. "Well," he
said, "I suppose the reason I am reacting this way is that
I was born and raised in a Christian home; my parents
were missionaries in China. All my life I have been running
away from God, but everywhere I go he pursues me." God
has been called, with reverent affection, "the Hound of
Heaven" because of his relentless pursuit of his own. That
is exactly what he was doing with Manasseh.

But Manasseh was determined to silence the voice of
God, and the only way he could silence that voice was to
silence the prophets: "Moreover, Manasseh shed very
much innocent blood until he had filled Jerusalem from
one end to another . . ."

Josephus, the Jewish historian, reports that he "slew all
the righteous men that were among the Hebrews, nor
would he spare the prophets, for he every day slew some
of them until Jerusalem was overflown with blood." There

is a very substantial and long-lasting Jewish and Christian tradition that it was during this time that Manasseh sealed Isaiah in a hollow oak tree and had him sawn in two. This may be the incident behind the reference in Hebrews 11 to men of faith, some of whom were "sawn asunder." Manasseh slew the prophets. He didn't want to hear the voice of God. So he

> . . . shed very much innocent blood until he had filled Jerusalem from one end to another; besides his sin with which he made Judah sin, in doing evil in the sight of the Lord (2 Kings 21:16).

Do you know that both the author of 2 Kings and Jeremiah affirm that it was because of the sins of Manasseh that the nation of Judah was taken captive? Only fifty years after Manasseh's death, the nation went into the Babylonian captivity, and Manasseh was responsible.

> Now the rest of the acts of Manasseh and all that he did and his sin which he committed, are they not written in the Book of the Chronicles of the Kings of Judah? And Manasseh slept with his fathers and was buried in the garden of his own house, in the garden of Uzza, and Amon his son became king in his place (2 Kings 21:17–18).

I remember the first time I read that passage. I thought, "That's strange! Here is a man who thumbed his nose at God for sixty-seven years, dying a ripe old age in his own bed in peace—the most wicked king in Judah's history, and God did nothing! He reigned longer than any other king in the history of Israel or Judah. Didn't you see, God? Weren't you aware of what was going on? Can a person really live that way and get away with it?"

A Ring in His Nose

But the entire story of Manasseh's life is not given to us in 2 Kings. The purpose of this book is to show us the precipitous decline of the nation. Many events in the lives of these kings were passed by for that reason. But the account is resumed and supplemented in 2 Chronicles 33. The first nine verses in the chapter is a restatement of the first nine verses of 2 Kings 21, almost verbatim. Then in verses 9 through 11:

> Thus Manasseh misled Judah and the inhabitants of Jerusalem to do more evil than the nations whom the Lord destroyed before the sons of Israel. And the Lord spoke to Manasseh and his people, but they paid no attention. [This is a briefer account of the ministry of the prophets to Manasseh and the people.] *Therefore* [emphasis mine] the Lord brought the commanders of the army of the king of Assyria against them, and they captured Manasseh with hooks, bound him with bronze *chains*, and took him to Babylon [Babylon was a province of Assyria at this time] (2 Chron. 33:9–11).

This mighty king of Judah, with a ring in his nose and chains on his hands and feet, was dragged off to a Babylonian dungeon! This is one of a number of Old Testament accounts for which we have excellent secular historical confirmation. To get the history of this period straight, recall that Sennacherib was the Assyrian king who twice invaded Judah during Hezekiah's reign. After the debacle recorded in 2 Kings 19, Sennacherib never returned to Judah. His loss of 168,000 men to tiny Judah was humiliating. Strangely, he records this final invasion of Judah as a great victory for Assyria. One recalls the words of Pyrrhus:

"One more such victory and I am lost." In any case, Sennacherib never again ventured into Judah's territory. He died in 680 B.C., a date that interestingly enough corresponds to the traditional date of Isaiah's martyrdom. It may be that Manasseh's inhumanity to the prophet was the final straw. When Sennacherib died he was succeeded by Esarhaddon who, I believe, was God's instrument of judgment to Manasseh. Esarhaddon, Sennacherib's successor, was a young, ambitious, militaristic sovereign spoiling for conquest. And six years after his coronation he invaded Syria-Palestine and took Manasseh to Babylon. In his great prism, now displayed at the London Museum he records that "twenty-two kings" (in the west) hearkened to him (were made tributary to Assyria) and of these was "Manasseh, king of Judah." Esarhaddon bound him with bronze chains and dragged him off to Babylon where for twelve years he languished in a dungeon.

That is the process God uses to bring us around. He will hem us in on every side with every witness to the truth. But if we refuse to listen, he will let us have our way. He will take his hands off us, and we will reap what we have sown; thus we enslave ourselves and are brought to the end of ourselves.

Repentance

But look closely at verse 12:

> And when he was in distress [the Hebrew says, "when he was hemmed in," i.e., when he was in such extremity that he had no place to turn], he entreated the Lord his God and humbled himself greatly before the God of his fathers (2 Chron. 33:12).

He entreated *his* God. He had lost his rule, but he hadn't lost his relationship. Jehovah was still *his* God. God intends for us to reign in life, to live in victory over every habit and every circumstance of life. But when we rebel against him, we lose our capacity to rule, and we become enslaved to our circumstances and to our passions and desires. But we never lose our relationship to him if we are truly his. So when Manasseh hit rock bottom, he turned to the Lord his God and humbled himself greatly before the God of his fathers. He said, "Lord, I am sunk. I am beat, I've had it. I am to blame. I have sinned." Josephus says that he "esteemed himself to be the cause of it all." He saw that he had no one else to blame. The problem was not his circumstances, nor the culture in which he lived. He had had every advantage. The problem was his own rebellious heart. He came to the place where he was willing to submit that heart to the Lord. He humbled himself greatly before the Lord his God.

> When he prayed to Him, He [God] was moved by his entreaty and heard his supplication, and brought him again to Jerusalem to his kingdom. Then Manasseh knew that the Lord *was* [the] God (2 Chron. 33:13).

God may have to chasten, because he chastens those whom he loves. He may have to discipline. He may bring hardship into our lives because of our rebellion. But he sees us as righteous in Jesus Christ. There is no sin that you can ever commit which will disqualify you in God's sight. You are forgiven! God never stops loving. He never stops accepting.

And so when Manasseh prayed, the Lord "heard his supplication and brought him again to Jerusalem to his kingdom." He was restored to his place of authority. And that is what God does with us. We don't have to work our way back into his acceptance. We don't have to prove that we are acceptable. We walk in a forgiven state; Paul says, "In Him [Christ] we have redemption through His blood, the forgiveness of our trespasses, according to the riches of His grace" (Eph. 1:7). And we can never, never, look back on the past and say that anything we have done disqualifies us. We are clean. We are forgiven. We are righteous in God's eyes.

Then, verse 13 says that Manasseh knew that the Lord was literally *the* God. He realized that those idols had nothing for him—there was only one Yahweh. You see, God uses even our sin, the most degrading sin that we could commit, in a redemptive way to show us that he is the Lord. The process is painful, but it is productive. Then Manasseh *knew* that the Lord was *the* God.

Rebuilding the Walls

Verses 14 through 17 are a record of Manasseh's activities in Jerusalem after his kingdom was restored to him: "Now after this he built the outer wall of the city of David on the west side of Gihon, in the valley, even to the entrance of the Fish Gate; and he encircled the Ophel *with it* and made it very high."

He rebuilt and strengthened the wall and the fortress that protected the city on the east and the southeast, overlooking the Kidron Valley. Evidently this was the place where the Assyrians had earlier breached the wall when he was taken into captivity. So he went back to that weak spot in the city's defenses and reinforced it.

"Then he put army commanders in all the fortified cities

of Judah." He placed contingents of soldiers with commanders in each of the fortified cities in the outlying
districts. He set his defenses out beyond the walls of
Jerusalem so that he would not be surprised again by an
attack at the wall.

"He also removed the foreign gods and the idol from
the house of the Lord, as well as all the altars which he
had built on the mountain of the house of the Lord and
in Jerusalem, and he threw them outside the city." He
purged the city of idolatry. He took every Asherah, every
Baal, and threw them out of the city. He wanted nothing
more to do with them.

"And he set up the altar of the Lord and sacrificed peace
offerings and thank offerings on it; and he ordered Judah
to serve the Lord God of Israel." He rebuilt the altar that
he had destroyed, and he offered peace and thank offerings
—the two offerings which have to do with our relationship
with God—peace because we have been reconciled to him,
and thanksgiving, which grows out of that reconciliation.

These are the marks of true repentance. If one is truly
repentant of sins he has committed, he will rebuild the
areas of weakness and strengthen them. He will guard
against surprise assaults in areas where he has been defeated before. He will move his defenses out beyond the
point of weakness. He will "make no provision for the
flesh." And he will deal with every vestige of idolatry in
his life. Every false god will come under judgment and be
cast out of the domain. And he will make Jesus Christ
Lord.

Note the parallel with Paul's statement in 2 Corinthians 7, in which he contrasts godly sorrow and worldly
sorrow:

> I now rejoice, not that you were made sorrowful, but that you were made sorrowful to *the point* of repentance; for you were made sorrowful according to *the will* of God, in order that you might not suffer loss in anything through us. For the sorrow that is according to *the will of* God produces a repentance without regret, *leading* to salvation, but the sorrow of the world produces death. For behold what earnestness this very thing, this godly sorrow, has produced in you, what vindication of yourselves, what indignation, what fear, what longing, what zeal, what avenging of wrong. In everything you demonstrated yourselves to be innocent in the matter (2 Cor. 7:9–11).

Worldly sorrow, he says, produces death. Worldly sorrow is the sorrow one has because he has been caught in sin or has reaped what he has sown. That is a sorrow over the consequences of sin but not remorse for the actual deed. That is regret without repentance, and it produced despair and depression. But there is a godly sorrow. There is a "sorrow to the point of repentance," Paul says. That repentance is revealed by a determination to clear oneself. He says, "Behold what earnestness . . . this godly sorrow has produced in you, what vindication of yourselves, what indignation, what fear, what longing, what zeal, what avenging of wrong!" That is, "You have determined to do what is right." That is a godly sorrow. Manasseh had that kind of sorrow. He dealt not only with his idolatrous spirit, he moved out into *every* area of life to deal with all causes of rebellion.

Verses 18 through 20 give us the final word on his life:

> Now the rest of the acts of Manasseh, even his prayer to his God, and the words of the seers who spoke to

him in the name of the Lord God of Israel, behold,
they are among the records of the kings of Israel. His
prayer also and *how* God was entreated by him, and
all his sin, his unfaithfulness, and the sites on which
he built high places and erected the Asherim and the
carved images, before he humbled himself, behold,
they are written in the records of the Hozai [the prophets or the seers whose writings evidently are the basis
for many of our prophetic books]. So Manasseh slept
with his fathers, and they buried him in his own house.
And Amon his son became king in his place (2 Chron.
33:18–20).

God gave him twenty more years of rule—ten years with
his father, thirteen years of wickedness, twelve years in a
dungeon, and twenty years of righteous rule. He became
one of the mighty kings of Judah.

There are a number of striking things in this biography.
First, we can identify with Manasseh because God could
write "Manasseh" over each of our lives. We have all
sinned as he sinned. Second, we can see something of the
process that God uses to bring us to repentance. But most
important, these passages speak of the completeness of the
forgiveness of God. Manasseh was notorious in Israel. He
was an evil, wicked man. And yet God reestablished him
on his throne. He was fully forgiven. He lived in power and
authority throughout the rest of his years.

Do you know what Manasseh's name means in Hebrew?
"Forgotten." That is the name that God wrote over his
sordid past and yours. Your sins are forgotten.

"Your sins and your lawless deeds I will remember no
more."

—8—

The Great Exchange

We've been exploring the New Covenant in the Old Testament. I hope you have gained in the process a new appreciation for the Old Testament and a desire to pursue with greater intensity your studies in that portion of the Bible. It is my belief that the Old Testament depicts in symbol, and history the basic truths that the New Testament teaches in a more abstract way. In other words the two books are complementary. One cannot understand the Old Testament without the New, nor the New without the Old. Since it is a generally accepted fact that a picture leaves a deeper impress on the mind than abstractions, the graphic Old Testament portrayal of truths taught in the New Testament will, unquestionably, round out our understanding of the full council of God.

With that thought in mind, I would like now to turn to the prophets for another example of Old Testament teaching on the New Covenant. We could observe this process in any number of Old Testament passages, however, there is one in which it is uniquely treated, I believe, and that is the 40th chapter of Isaiah. May I suggest that before you read further you do some advance study in that remarkable prophecy and observe for yourself Isaiah's approach to this crucial subject.

Now, assuming that you have done your homework, let's take a look at Isaiah's instruction.

The Angle of Vision

In order to understand this prophecy we need to understand something of its setting both in the Book of Isaiah and in history. It is always important to establish both the literary and historical context of any portion of the Bible, but this is particularly important when we study the Old Testament.

First a word about the setting of the chapter with reference to the entire Book of Isaiah. Isaiah's prophecy, it's generally agreed, falls into three clearly defined divisions. The first section (chapters 1–35) is set against the Assyrian Period and in particular during the period 680–640 B.C. This was the time when both Israel and Judah were locked in a desperate struggle with the Assyrian Empire. It was during this period that Samaria fell and the Northern Kingdom of Israel went into captivity. Isaiah was God's spokesman during this period to the Judean kings, Jotham, Ahaz, and Hezekiah.

The second section of Isaiah (chapters 36–39) is a prose description of the final years of King Hezekiah of Judah and contains in particular a prediction of the Babylonian captivity by the prophet Isaiah. It seems to me that one inference drawn from this section is that one can live too long! Chapter 38 tells us that Hezekiah became mortally ill and was told by the prophet that he would die, whereupon he pled for extra years of life. The Lord gave him his request but quite frankly sent leanness into his soul—or at least the soul of the nation. During those extra fifteen years he sired the wicked Manasseh. This deed in itself was disastrous to the future course of the nation. But for his next act he truly outdid himself! Merodach-baladan, the king of Babylon, having sent a get-well card (39:1) was invited to Hezekiah's court. Babylon at this period in history was no threat to Judah being a minor principality, tributary to Assyria. Hezekiah, reacting in the grandiose style typical of most oriental monarchs, showed Merodach-baladan "all his treasure house, the silver and the gold and the spices and the precious oil and his whole armory and all that was found in his treasures. There was nothing in his house, nor in all his dominion, that Hezekiah did not show him." In short he gave away all Judah's secrets. And Isaiah's astonished response was that Hezekiah's perfidy would be the end of them all (39:6). Which, in fact, it was. Merodach-baladan evidently determined to sack Jerusalem if he ever conquered the west. Some 100 years later, Nebuchadnezzar who presumably had access to his records did it for him. As Isaiah predicted, all that Hezekiah's fathers had laid up in store was carried away into Babylon and nothing was left (v. 6). It is against this background that Isaiah 40–66 is written. Isaiah, anticipating the Babylonian exile, writes words of comfort to these captives. In other words, he anticipates the exile and writes words of comfort addressed to them in these circumstances—100 years before the event. How like the Lord to anticipate their need and raise up a spokesman, whose works would be waiting for them when they arrived in Babylon.

It is this fact, of course, that has caused the critics to propose a second Isaiah—a Deutero-Isaiah—who ministered during the exilic period. So precise are his predictions, they reason, that Isaiah from his 8th century B.C.

vantage point could never have so exactly anticipated their circumstances. Vocabulary and style, they say, show two authors, but quite frankly in my opinion it is their bias that is showing. The real problem is unbelief in the supernatural origin of Scripture. Certainly an omniscient God can so act and so instruct his prophets to act that real prediction is possible. It is true there are stylistic differences between the first and last divisions of the book, but no more than you would expect in the writings of one whose ministry spanned forty years or so. I've often wondered what the results would be of subjecting the writings of the great Old Testament scholar William F. Albright to the same sort of literary analysis. His writings spanned a comparable forty-year period. I suspect we might find there is a Deutero-Albright. The issue, of course, is much too complex to go into here. But it is my belief that the critics are wrong. There is one author of both "books" of Isaiah, Isaiah, ben Amoz. (It's worth noting, in passing, that Jesus did, too. Compare Jesus' word about the authorship of the two quotations from Isaiah, one from each "book," in John 12: 36–40.)

In any case we need to be certain about the background of Isaiah 40. It is cast against the tragic events of the Babylonian captivity and is addressed to the captives of that exile who had been deported into Babylon. It is, therefore, a word of comfort to captives.

One further word about the historical backdrop of Isaiah 40. It is good to fix firmly in your mind the actual condition of these people. Fortunately we know quite a lot about their plight both from biblical and from classical sources. As a result of three successive deportations (in 605 B.C., 597 B.C., and 586 B.C.) a small number of Judeans were taken into exile and located near Babylon on the River Chebar. The Chebar (called the Kibarru by the Babylonians) was an artificial irrigation ditch or aquaduct that branched off the Euphrates north of Babylon. The exiles, we know, were located in what amounted to refugee camps close by Babylon where Babylonian officialdom could keep its eyes on them. The Hebrews were a pesky lot, given to rebellion and treachery and therefore they wanted to keep them under surveillance. It seems that they enjoyed a degree of freedom, were able to travel in a limited sense, certainly having access to the city of Babylon. In fact, many of them worked there as domestic servants in Babylonian households. We need to bear in mind that these Judeans were not of servant stock. Almost all of them came from the noble class, were business and professional people, artisans and the like. Now they were reduced to lower class status living in the shadow of the great city of Babylon and serving Babylonian nobility.

Now a word about Babylon itself. We are again fortunate to have what amounts to an eyewitness description by the Greek historian Heroditus who wrote some fifty years after the fall of Babylon. The city itself was not destroyed by the Persians so what Heroditus describes was virtually the city the exiles observed. Heroditus tells us that Babylon was enclosed by a great wall some 300 feet tall. More recent observations by excavators make the figure more like 85 feet tall suggesting that Heroditus' figures were a bit exaggerated. However, by any comparison Babylon's walls were impressive. Actually, there is no analogy for them anywhere else in the Ancient Near East. Babylon was unique. Heroditus tells us further that a four-horse chariot could be driven around the top of the walls thus making possible swift deployment of troops. The walls were surrounded by a great moat filled by the Euphrates.

The Euphrates, by the way, flowed directly under the walls of the city from north to south, thus the city always had adequate water supply in times of siege. The tunnel under the walls through which the river flowed was protected by great bronze doors. There were no war machines at that time that could breach the mighty walls of Babylon. As the saying is, Babylon had it made. They were invincible.

Entrance into the city was by great tower gates, likewise heavily fortified. Each of these gates was dedicated to one of the gods of the Babylonian pantheon. If one walked around the circumference of the walls in a clockwise manner, he would encounter in turn the gates of Ishtar—the goddess of sex and fertility, Sin (pronounced Seen) the moon god, Marduk—the patron god of Babylon, Enlil—identified with the god, Bel, the Lord of the World, Urash—the god of war, Shamash, the sun god, and Hadad, the storm god. If you entered by the Ishtar gate, you would be confronted by a broad processional way leading to the great ziggurat of Babylon and the temple of Marduk. The ziggurat, called by the Babylonians Etemenanki ("The Foundation of Heaven and Earth") was an enormous structure, some 300 feet tall standing, most likely, on the actual site of the original Tower of Babel. Everywhere one looked he would be confronted with a dazzling array of temples and shrines dedicated to pagan gods and goddesses. We are told that there were fifty-three such temples located within the walled city.

The Processional Way itself was dedicated to Marduk, the patron god of Babylon. On the beveled sides of the limestone paving slabs one could read "To the honor of Marduk." If you walked down that great highway, 65 feet wide, over 1,000 feet long, each step would bring you again and again in confrontation with those words, TO THE HONOR OF MARDUK . . . TO THE HONOR OF MARDUK . . . TO THE HONOR OF MARDUK. The Processional Way was lined with enameled bricks, bearing symbols of Marduk and Ishtar. Everywhere, inescapably, you would be overwhelmed by the worship of idols.

Nebuchadnezzar's palace, located to the west of the Ishtar gate, was itself a mute testimony to the grandeur and power of Babylon. It was an enormous complex of buildings, actually a fortress built to protect the king and his courtiers. The walls were almost 150 feet thick. (It sems that Nebuchadnezzar added an extra 23 feet of bricks to further protect himself since in this later addition every brick bears his name.) In any case one could never get away from the fact that Nebuchadnezzar and his gods were ruling securely.

Now do you understand the plight of the exiles? Badly in need of encouragement, they were confronted inescapably with the glory and the might of the idols and the obvious ease and prosperity of the Babylonians.

Marduk ruled! The Gentiles were at ease. While off to the west their city lay in ruins, their temple was a blackened shell. And they could justifiably ask, "Where is the God of Israel?" "What of the promises given to the Patriarchs?" "Where is the justice that is due us?" It is against this dreary background, now, that Isaiah's prophecies are cast.

Comfort for Captives

> Comfort, O comfort My people, says your God.
> Speak kindly to Jerusalem;
> and call out to her,
> that her warfare has ended,

that her iniquity has been removed,
that she has received of the Lord's hand
double for all her sins (Isa. 40:1–2).

The Hebrew says, rather picturesquely, "Speak to the *heart* of Israel." (Have you ever been disconsolate and someone tried to comfort you by speaking to your head?) God may at first speak to the mind because he does want us to get the facts straight. But he never leaves the matter there. His ultimate intention is to address the heart because that is the place where all issues are ultimately resolved. God wants our hearts to be untroubled (John 14:1), and so he proposes to speak to Israel's heart and comfort her.

Now from what will the exiles derive comfort? Three great facts—the first, "her warfare has ended." Or, more in keeping with the idea of the prophet, "her servitude as a result of warfare has ended." Israel had been mastered. They had lost the war and found themselves in bondage to their conquerors. But that captivity was coming to an end. Her warfare had ended. Second, her iniquity had been paid for. And finally, she had received from the Lord double for all her sins.

Our English translation, unfortunately, gives the impression that Israel had suffered twice as much as she deserved and thus had atoned for her sins. The statement, "She has received . . . double for all her sins" could lead to that erroneous conclusion. However, the phrase is actually, "she has received a *doubling* for her sins"—an expression possibly rooted in social custom. It appears that in ancient times debtors who failed to pay their bills were publicly humiliated. If someone failed to pay his Bank Assyria Card, the due bill was posted on his front gate with appropriate ceremony. Imagine the embarrassment! But let's suppose that our unfortunate debtor has a friend who will pay the debt for him. In which case, the friend, having discharged the debt, can then *double over* the bill, thus securing freedom from further harassment and embarrassment. The fact of the debt and the amount of it are hidden from prying eyes. The ex-debtor is now free from liability and shame. What a relief—what a comfort!

This, then, is the word of comfort to Israel. The score has been settled. The debt has been paid. Their shame and servitude is removed. They are free. And is not that our experience as well in Christ? He has "doubled over" our sins—paid for them, hidden them from view. What a comfort!

The cross, done in time, eternal in its implications, did that for both Old and New Israel. "In him [Christ] we have redemption through his blood, the forgiveness of our trespasses according to the riches of his grace which he lavished upon us" (Eph. 1:7, 8) . How comforting to know that he will remember our sins and iniquities no more (Jer. 31:34) .

You Are That Man

There are few things as bad in life as being fingered as the guilty party. If it's ever happened to you, you know what I'm talking about. It happened once to King David.

They tell me that in the spring a young man's fancy turns to what the young women have been thinking about all year. However, in ancient Israel at that season of the year, men's thoughts turned to war, or so it says in 2 Samuel 11:1. David's kingdom was at war with the Ammonites, and the young men went off to fight that spring. David, however, had other fish to fry, and so stayed behind in Jerusalem. He made the wrong mistake, as they say. It

happened one day as he was walking on the roof of his
house overlooking Jerusalem that his roving eye lighted
upon a young and very beautiful woman—bathing. (One
wonders at her naïveté. After all, David was a handsome
fellow. In addition, since Bathsheba was the wife of Uriah,
one of David's closest friends, they must have met at state
and social occasions.) In any case, David inquired about
her (evidently, he did not recognize her), learned that
she was someone's wife (that should have been the end
of that!), and furthermore, that she was the wife of Uriah
his friend.

However, there was no stopping David now. As the account tells us, he "sent messengers, and took her; and he
lay with her. Then she returned to her house." And David
thought he had covered his tracks and that the affair was
undetected. And so it was—except God saw it. A few
weeks later Bathsheba announced her plight, "I am with
child" (v. 5). David panicked. Uriah was off fighting a
war. Anyone could put two and two together (or count
up to nine), and so David was in big trouble. The kings
of Israel, unlike the sovereigns of other nations at that
time, were subject to the Law. There was no distinction
between king and subject in Israel. Everyone was a subject.
All sat under the judgment of the Law, and David knew
that his good reputation, if not his life, was over.

Now you can read the rest of the sordid episode on your
own. David tried to contrive a scheme whereby the guilt
could be lifted from him, but every attempt ended in
futility. Finally, in blind frustration, David ordered the
murder of his friend Uriah. Now, with the only contrary
witness to the deed silenced, David was free to take Bathsheba as his wife and thus is now home free. Ah, but "the
thing that David had done displeased the Lord." Alas,

David's guilt-ridden heart had already indicted him (read Ps. 32). Now Nathan's allegorical tale gave another turn to the screw.

> There were two men in one city, the one rich and the other poor. The rich man had a great many flocks and herds. But the poor man had nothing except one little ewe lamb which he bought and nourished; and it grew up together with him and his children. It would eat his bread and drink of his cup, and lie in his bosom, and was like a daughter to him. Now a traveler came to the rich man, and he was unwilling to take from his own flock or his own herd to prepare for the wayfarer who had come to him; rather he took the poor man's ewe lamb and prepared it for the man who had come to him (2 Sam. 12:1-4).

David was incensed. "As the Lord lives, the man who has done this deserves to die; and he shall restore the lamb fourfold, because he did this thing, and because he had no pity" (v. 5). Nathan pointed his long bony finger at David and said, "You are the man." The ruse was over. God's relentless love had found David out. As someone has said, the only place we are free from the perturbations of God's love is in hell. Then David said to Nathan, "I have sinned against the Lord." And Nathan said to David, "The Lord also has taken away your sin; you shall not die." Thus David wrote:

> How blessed is he whose transgression is forgiven, whose sin is covered!
> How blessed is the man to whom the Lord does not impute iniquity, and in whose spirit there is no deceit!

> When I kept silent about my sin, my body wasted away
>   through my groaning all day long.
> For day and night Thy hand was heavy upon me;
>   my vitality was drained away as with the fever-heat
>   of summer.
> Therefore, let everyone who is godly pray to Thee in a
>   time when Thou mayest be found; surely in a flood
>   of great waters they shall not reach him.
> Thou art my hiding place;
>   Thou dost preserve me from trouble;
>   Thou dost surround me with songs of deliverance
>   (Ps. 32:1-4, 6, 7).

David was an adulterer, a murderer, a liar, and worse—he was forgiven. It's true he bore the consequences of the sin in his life for years to come. His baby son died, his household erupted into revolt and violence, and he temporarily lost control of his kingdom. Sin always leaves ugly marks. However, David's relationship with God was not impaired. He was free from that spirit of guilt and condemnation that is so spiritually draining and debilitating. God was "at home" to him. He was restored to fellowship with the Father.

Do you likewise feel defiled? So many Christians live with a nagging sense of guilt based on past failure. They feel that God has rejected them and turned away. I have a friend who told me once he was afraid to look at the face of God because he knew God would frown at him. Do you feel that way? I walked through my backyard the other day on my way to my office and my five-year-old son said, "Dad, is everything okay?" I replied, "Sure, son, why do you ask?" He responded, "Well, you didn't smile at me." (Needless to say, I did then.) Do you know everything is okay? Do you know you're okay? God is smiling at you. He has forgotten your sins and iniquities. *"Rejoice,* your names are written in heaven." That is a word of comfort!

Make Way for the Glory

And now Isaiah hears another comforting voice.

> A voice is calling, clear the way for the Lord in the
> wilderness; make smooth in the desert a highway for
> our God.
> Let every valley be lifted up, and every mountain and
> hill be made low;
> and let the rough ground become a plain,
> And the rugged terrain a broad valley;
> Then the glory of the Lord will be revealed,
>   and all flesh shall see it together;
> for the mouth of the Lord has spoken (Isa. 40:4–5).

This passage also is rooted in oriental custom. In those days when a monarch traveled from place to place, he sent ahead teams of workmen whose task it was to "clear the way" for the king. They leveled out the rough places, filled the valleys, and made cuts through the mountains so the kings could travel in comfort and safety.

Heroditus tells a story about Cyrus when he was approaching Babylon. It seems that one of his prize horses was swept away by the Gynges River, whereupon he devoted an entire summer and his army to taming this great torrent. He did so by digging several hundred diversion channels thus breaking up the river into a number of smaller rivulets through which he could pass in safety and go on his way. I've often wondered what his army thought about such nonsense. However, the effort expended was in keeping with the customs of the time. The king traveled like royalty. No time or effort was spared to "clear his way."

Now it is clearly this practice that Isaiah has in mind in verses 3–5. The king, in this case, however, is Messiah. The voice pleads with the Judean captives to clear the way for Messiah, the king, to set up his rule in the nation in exile. Some interpreters prefer to make this symbol describe the journey back to the land. It seems to me, however, to refer to the need for a spiritual awakening on the part of the exiles *where they are.* If in their depressed state they will make room in their lives for the King, he will display his glory there—in exile. Israel thought in terms of the glory returning to Jerusalem. They reasoned that when a return became possible, they would reconstruct the temple and then the Shekinah—the cloud by day and pillar of fire by night, the symbol of God's presence in the nation— would reappear over that temple. But the voice promises that the glory would be revealed there in Babylon first. It is true that these exiles did return and rebuild. And the glory (in the person of Jesus) did appear in that temple but I do not believe that is the primary reference of this passage. Isaiah's concern is the revelation of Yahweh's glory in captivity. The voice, of course, speaks symbolically. The actual Shekinah never appeared in exile. That truth, however, could be experienced in a spiritual sense. When the exiles' lives were subject to Messiah, the King, they would amongst their captives begin to display the glory of God. Their lives would reflect his character. Do you see the issue? On every hand there were temples and idols dedicated to the most perverse and kinky practices. It was the Lord's plan that there be lives in the midst of this awful scene devoted to his lordship—reflecting his right- eousness—revealing his glory.

The New Testament writers, with inspired insight, applied this passage to the ministry of John the Baptist. His role, as Isaiah's, was to prepare the people spiritually for Messiah's coming. From the wilderness regions near Jericho he called Israel to readiness, "The King is coming. Clear the way." Remove the conditions of heart that impede his progress—the pride, smugness, indifference that made it impossible for the Lord to gain access to the hearts of his people. John's choice of locale for his ministry was deliberate. The wilderness of Jordan, like the wilderness of Babylon, symbolized the heart of Israel—barren and wasted. What could be more descriptive—of their hearts—and ours. We, like Israel, must prepare the way for the King, remove every barrier to his entrance in and rule over our lives. *Then* the glory of the Lord will be revealed in our circumstances, our captivity. As we move among our contemporaries every step will declare our lives to be TO THE HONOR OF JESUS . . . TO THE HONOR OF JESUS . . . TO THE HONOR OF JESUS.

The Arm of the Lord

> Get yourself up on a high mountain,
> > O Zion, bearer of good news,
> Lift up your voice mightily,
> > O Jerusalem, bearer of good news;
> Lift it up, do not fear.
> > Say to the cities of Judah,
> "Here is your God!"
> > Behold the Lord God will come with might,
> With His arm ruling for Him.
> > Behold, His reward is with Him,
> And His recompense before Him.
> > Like a shepherd He will tend His flock,

> In His arm He will gather the lambs,
>   And carry them in His bosom;
> He will gently lead the nursing ewes (Isa. 40:9–11).

In this scene, Judah is pictured as delivered from her oppressors. Having returned to the Lord she is now returned to her land. And as a returnee is charged with an evangelistic task. She is to declare the truth of the Lord's presence to the smaller towns of Judah. The substance of her message is "Behold your God." The essence of it follows (vv. 10, 11).

Yahweh is described as a conquering hero who bears his mighty arm in indignation and wrath. His arm "rules" for him (v. 10). The monuments of this period almost always portray the kings with their right arm flexed. They always remind me of the muscle builder advertisements that promise to make a man out of you in thirty days or less. Somewhere on the ad there is a picture of some massive young man with upraised twenty-one-inch biceps who used to be as skinny as I. Alas, it never quite worked for me. At least never to the promised degree. Thus somewhere in my youth I adopted the policy that since I couldn't produce a twenty-one-inch biceps, I should align myself with someone who could—a policy that had some obvious drawbacks. Unfortunately, might does not always, if ever, make things right—unless it is the might of our sovereign Lord. It seems to me that that clearly is the symbol in view here. God's arm is a picture of his mighty energy and power when he comes as king and judge of the earth.

Ah, but did you notice as you read this passage that the same arm with which he deals crushing blows to the nations is the arm that encircles us in love! The same arm that is lifted in vengeance against his enemies is the arm that gathers the lambs and carries them in his bosom. The arm of the king is the arm of the shepherd. The power of that mighty arm is stretched out to enfold his people in love and tenderness. Again—what a relief, what a comfort!

Now observe the power of that arm (vv. 12 ff.) .

> Who has measured the waters in the hollow of his
> hand?

Two-thirds of the surface of the earth is water—God measures it up in the palm of his hand.

> And marked off the heavens by the span?

A span is the distance between the end of the thumb and the little finger—about seven to nine inches. God has so measured the heavens. Not only is he immense, but he is precise.

> And calculated the dust of the earth by the measure?
>   [A measure is about two gallons.]
> And weighed the mountains in a balance,
>   and the hills in a pair of scales?
> Who has directed the Spirit of the Lord,
>   or as his counselor has informed him?
> With whom did he consult and who gave him
>   understanding?
> And who taught him in the path of justice and
>   taught him knowledge,
>   and informed him of the way of understanding?

Do you understand? God has everything we need. In him are hidden all the treasures of wisdom and knowledge

(Col. 2:3). This was a period of history characterized by apparently wise and powerful men. Some of the greatest monarchs of history ruled in this age. Men who were absolute in their sovereignty. Also this was roughly the period of Buddha, Confucius, and Zoroaster. This was shortly before the Golden Age of Greece. The names of men like Euripides, Sophocles, and Pericles were soon to become household words. Men from all over the civilized world went to the Delphic Oracle in Greece to receive answers to complex questions (and I might add receive complex answers). However, God declares he has received no counsel from these sources. They have added nothing to him. May I add that history certainly reinforces this truth. There is a famous story of Croesus the Lydian king that always cracks me up. It seems he endowed the Delphic Oracle with certain funds for which favor he was awarded a season's ticket to the Olympic Games (it's true!) and a lifetime membership in the Oracle. When about to go to war with the Persians, he inquired of the Oracle whether he ought to fight or capitulate. The Oracle with characteristic ambiguity informed him that if he went to war with Persia, he would destroy a kingdom. Thus encouraged, he waged battle with Cyrus only to discover that it was his own empire, Lydia, which he destroyed. So much for the Delphic Oracle.

> Behold, the nations are like a drop from a bucket,
> [the drops that cling to the bottom of a water skin]
>   and are regarded as a speck of dust on the scales;
> Behold, he lifts up the islands like fine dust.
> [the "islands" were the Mediterranean coastlands]
> Even Lebanon is not enough to burn, nor its
>   beasts enough for a burnt offering.

If one offered a sacrifice appropriate to the character of God, he could offer all of the animals of Lebanon or all the wood of that great forest, and that offering would not be adequate.

> All the nations are as nothing before him,
>> they are regarded by him as less than nothing
>> and meaningless (Isa. 40:12–17).

All Wisdom and Power

Do you understand what Isaiah is saying? God has infinite wisdom and infinite power. Wisdom and power are the attributes we seek above all others. We rate our fellow men by their ability to display these two attributes—wisdom and power. We look at intelligence and influence and we are impressed. Isaiah informs us that God is the source of both wisdom and power. God's estimate of our might is, "nothing . . . less than nothing . . . meaningless." The expression "less than nothing" actually signifies in Hebrew thought the point at which a thing ceases to be. The great empires of Isaiah's age and ours—nothing. Wisdom and power exist solely in him.

The Incomparable God

You noticed, I'm sure, that verses 18 through 25 are bracketed by the phrase, "To whom then will you liken me?" This section, then, contains a series of comparisons, the point of which is to declare that God is incomparable. First he takes on idols and dismisses them peremptorily. (Note the irony of the last line of verse 20, "To prepare an idol that will not totter.")

> Then he compares himself with man:
>> Do you not know? Have you not heard?

> Has it not been declared to you from the
>   beginning?
> Have you not understood from the foundations
>   of the earth?
> It is he who sits above the vault of the earth,
>   and its inhabitants are like grasshoppers;
> who stretches out the heavens like a curtain,
>   and spreads them out like a tent to dwell in.
> He it is who reduces rulers to nothing,
>   who makes the judges of the earth meaningless.
> Scarcely have they been planted,
>   scarcely have they been sown,
>   scarcely has their stock taken root in the earth,
> But he merely blows on them, and they wither,
>   and the storm carries them away like stubble (Isa.
>   40:21–24).

Where are the great men of past ages—where are Sargon I, Thutmosis III—the men of power and influence in the ancient East? They're gone. It is as though God blew on them and they disappeared. But God exists. He is the *incomparable* one—you cannot compare him with the works of man's hands, nor with man himself.

Look to the Stars

> But with what can you compare him?
>   "To whom then will you liken Me,
>   that I should be his equal?"
>   says the Holy One.
>   "Lift up your eyes on high" (Isa. 40:25–26).

Of all the animals, man's posture best suits him to look up; animals look down or back, but seldom up. The Greeks called man *anthropos*, the one who looks up. But the more civilized and cultured we become, the less we look up (smog, haze, and city lights make it difficult to see much anyway). However, primitive man could look up and see stars. And if he did so, he saw the heavens declaring the glory of God.

> Lift up your eyes on high
> and see who has created these stars.
> The One who leads forth their host by number,
> he calls them all by name;
> Because of the greatness of his might and the strength of his power
> not one of them is missing (Isa. 40:26).

In the ancient world the gods were identified with creation. (Anu *was* the heavens for instance.) Yahweh, however, is the *creator* of the heavens—transcendent above the stars, yet controlling each orbit and movement. The term here translated "missing" is akin to the Hebrew word for flock and actually means "to lag behind." Not one star in God's "flock" ever lags behind. What a striking picture! When God leads out the stars each evening, he doesn't leave any behind. There was never a time an ancient could look off to the east at sunset and observe that a star was missing—that one got left behind. God's control of the universe is absolute. Not one aspect of his creation is outside of his purview. His "sheep" hear his voice and he knows them and they follow him. Is God going to lose you? Can he forget your needs? Can he be preoccupied with some great cosmic event and thus overlook your need? Indeed he will not!

> Why do you say, O Jacob, and assert, O Israel,
> "My way is hidden from the Lord,
> and the justice due me escapes the notice
> of my God"? (Isa. 40:27).

Have you ever said that? Sure you have. So have I. "God, you've forgotten me. You're not aware of my needs. You're not doing right by me!" But if we understand that our God is the God who holds the universe together and orders the infinite details of it, then we will know that he is never indifferent to our needs nor unable to minister to them.

> Do you not know? Have you not heard?
> The everlasting God, the Lord, the creator of the
>   ends of the earth
>   does not become weary or tired.
> His understanding is inscrutable.
> He gives strength to the weary,
>   and to him who lacks might he increases power
>   (Isa. 40:28, 29).

The word for power is akin to the Hebrew word for "bone," and it means firmness. If you tend to cave in under pressure this passage says that to him who lacks might, he increases firmness. He puts starch in our backbone!

> Though youths grow weary and tired,
>   and vigorous young men stumble badly,
> Yet those who wait for the Lord
>   will gain new strength (Isa. 40:30, 31).

With Wings Like Eagles

How will we receive this power that we need so desperately? It is by acknowledging that we are "without might," and by waiting on the Lord. This passage actually says, "Those who wait for the Lord will *exchange* strength," affirming the same principle as Paul when he writes:

> I have been crucified with Christ;
> and it is no longer I who live,
> but Christ lives in me (Gal. 2:20).

Our natural resources will fail, young men in the vigor of youth will stumble and fall, the hardiest individuals will grow faint. But those who wait upon the Lord will gain new strength—exchange weakness for strength.

> They will mount up with wings like eagles,
> They will run and not get tired,
> They will walk and not become weary (Isa. 40:31).

I used to live in Texas, and we occasionally drove down to the Big Bend country, where the Rio Grande cuts through the St. Helena Canyon. I remember lying in the sun by the river bank and watching the eagles soar—seldom flapping their wings, rising effortlessly on the great thermals that develop in that canyon. I never saw one fall out of the sky. They are a picture of majesty and strength. They soar—and so will we! What a picture of effortless strength.

Second, "They will run and not get tired. They will walk and not become weary." Note the implied contrast with verse 29. "The youths grow weary and tired." Even the strong and the stout-hearted will be weakened by their exertion and fold. But those who wait on the Lord will renew their strength. They will run all day and not become tired. That's the word for those pressure-packed days when you want somebody to stop the world so you can get off. When you would press the panic button if you could just find it under the pile on your desk. That's the day you can run and not get tired, sustained by his inexhaustible strength.

Finally, "They will walk and not become weary." Here's the word for those dreary, monotonous, humdrum days when life gets so "daily." When the sink is full of dirty dishes and the kids are screaming and nobody seems to care. That is the day in which you can walk and not become weary supported by the mighty *Arm* of the Lord.

And you can do it—you can endure. When nobody sees or cares, when no one happens by to observe your need and strengthen you—if you're waiting on the Lord, you can run and not get tired; you can walk and not become weary. That is why David said, "How blessed is the man whose strength is in the Lord." Passing through the valley of Baca (the word means "weeping"), he makes it a place of springs; he goes "from strength to strength" (Ps. 84: 5-7).

The essence, the central core of the new and eternal covenant lies just here: in order to be strong, we must exchange our weakness for his strength. The God of the universe wants to swallow us up, and when he does, we will find that he supplies everything we need for any situation.

In C. S. Lewis' *The Silver Chair* (Collier Books), Jill found herself transported into a strange land because of her own pride and foolishness. She was lost and very thirsty, so she began to look for a stream. She found the stream, but she also found the Lion, Aslan, lying by the stream. The Lion told her if she was thirsty she could come and drink, and Lewis describes the voice:

> The voice was not like a man's. It was deeper, wilder, and stronger; a sort of heavy, golden voice . . .

> "May I . . . could I . . . would you mind going away while I [drink]?" said Jill.

The Lion answered this only by a look and a very low growl. And as Jill gazed at its motionless bulk, she realized that she might as well have asked the whole mountain to move aside for her convenience.

The delicious rippling noise of the stream was driving her nearly frantic.

"Will you promise not to—do anything to me, if I do come?" said Jill.

"I make no promise," said the Lion.

Jill was so thirsty now that, without noticing it, she had come a step nearer.

"Do you eat girls?" she said.

"I have swallowed up girls and boys, women and men, kings and emperors, cities and realms," said the Lion.

It didn't say this as if it were boasting, nor as if it were sorry, nor as if it were angry. It just said it.

"I daren't come and drink," said Jill.

"Then you will die of thirst," said the Lion.

"Oh, dear!" said Jill, coming another step nearer. "I suppose I must go and look for another stream then."

"There is no other stream," said the Lion.

If we allow ourselves to be swallowed up in what he is, we will know with Isaiah the joy of his strength in us. Why, in the face of this unrestricted offer, should we hang on for one moment to what can only betray us in the end? Isaiah teaches what the whole of the Bible sets forth: God eternally reaches out to us, to bring us peace—forgiveness and power through his Son. This is the New Covenant to which God has bound himself; the eternal promise of God.